Caramba's Revenge

A comedy

William Norfolk

Samuel French — London
New York - Toronto - Hollywood

© 1998 BY MARTIN APPLEBY

Please see page iv for further copyright information

CHARACTERS

Lottie, late 60s
Doris, late 60s
Marge, late 60s
Ronnie (short for Veronica), 20
Augustus Grubb, late 30s
Rose, 70s
Grace, 70s

The action of the play takes place in the living-room of a terraced house

Time: the present

SYNOPSIS OF SCENES

ACT I

ACT II

**Other plays by William Norfolk
published by Samuel French Ltd**

The Charlatan

Hunting Pink

The Lights Are Warm and Coloured

Old Quebec

ACT I

Scene 1

A Saturday in autumn. Noon

The scene is a much-lived-in, much cluttered living-room of a terraced house. In the back wall is a window overlooking a garden, or garden wall. There is also a doorway here to the kitchen, part of which is seen when the door is open. An exit leads from the kitchen to the garden. A door R leads to the stairs—visible when the door is open—and to the unseen front door. The furniture is utilitarian and well-worn, and includes a table, four chairs, a sideboard and a TV

The three old ladies who occupy the house, all of them approaching seventy—two of whom are present when the curtain rises—have the same hairstyle: cut straight to just below the ears, with a fringe descending almost to the eyebrows. Lottie's is a natural salt-and-pepper, whilst that of Marge is subtly mauve. Doris's is of a more positive colour: reddish auburn. Their clothes, which are clean and neat, cover a fashion period spanning forty years or so

Doris stands by the table, unloading her shopping trolley, while Lottie sits reading from an exercise book, occasionally correcting, or making notes

Lottie I finished chapter seven of my novel this morning.

Doris Nice. Pilchards have gone up fourpence.

Lottie Fourpence, old money?

Doris Ninepence ha'penny, old money.

Lottie Would you like me to read it to you?

Doris Ten per cent, give or take a fraction.

Lottie (*reading*) "Vanda Lane sat deep in thought, her shapely chin cupped in her delicate hands: her seductive silk-clad legs tucked demurely beneath her chair. She stood, smoothing her dress over her pale, alabaster thighs. 'Cast those luscious lamps over this, babe,' Tod Mallet ejaculated sardonically——"

Doris "Ejaculated"?

Lottie (*firmly*) Sardonically!

Doris The fish in these fish fingers is unspecified.

Lottie (*continuing to read*) "Vanda smiled, revealing a tantalising glimpse of perfectly matched teeth; and, tossing back her fiery golden locks, caught the last of the winter sun in them. Her bosom heaved with rampant emotion."

Pause

Why did Marge chuck you out of the kitchen?

Doris (*sighing*) She's experimenting again.

Lottie What is it this time?

Doris A pie, using three types of beans. She says they're cheap, and it'll be full of proteins, and things.

Lottie Farts, mainly. Let me help you with that. (*She crosses and helps unload the trolley*) You stopped for a port and lemon on the way back.

Doris I swear I——

Lottie You must spend a fortune on extra-strong mints.

Doris It's my——

Lottie If you're about to use the fallacious argument that you used your own money, you have no "own money". None of us have. That's what being part of a co-operative's all about. (*She picks up a small jar*) What's this?

Doris Caviare.

Lottie It says "lumpfish".

Doris The poor man's caviare. We've got to treat ourselves every now and then.

Lottie I hope this lemon doesn't indicate you're hoping to sneak a bottle of gin through the housekeeping accounts?

Doris It's to squeeze on the caviare. And if there's enough left over, it'll do as a beauty treatment for the hard skin on your elbows. Though, frankly, I think nothing short of paint stripper will shift that.

Lottie (*searching the bottom of the trolley*) What have you done with the gun?

Doris I didn't take it with me.

Lottie What if you'd been raped?

Doris I'd have asked him back for lunch.

Lottie And where's the receipt?

Doris I must have lost it.

Lottie Tut tut; no sense of accountability. (*She gets out a pocket calculator and tots up the items from the labels on them*) You'd lose your head if it wasn't screwed on, and what would you do then, without a mouth to pour all that booze into? The house is being watched.

Doris (*wearily*) Oh, Lottie: not again? That's the third time this——

Lottie A girl: about nineteen or twenty. Four pounds, twenty-seven. (*She holds out her hand for the change*)

Doris gives it to her. Lottie then proceeds to place it in a cash box, which she locks, and makes an entry in the accounts book

I saw her when I put the rubbish out. Sitting on the wall opposite. Casing the joint, obviously.

Doris Or waiting for a bus! (*She sighs*) I'll go and have a quick peep through the letter-box.

Lottie Is that advisable, dear? Last time you did that it took you a couple of days to fully straighten up.

Doris Very well: I'll go upstairs and look out of the window.

The kitchen door opens, and Marge emerges

Ah, Mrs Beeton's arrived. Nice to know the kitchen's no longer out of bounds.

Doris sweeps into the kitchen

We hear the sound of running water

Marge (*indicating the lumpfish*) What's this?

Lottie Lumpfish: the poor man's——

Marge I was questioning its presence: I'm perfectly aware what it is. It's the roe from an uncouth spiny-finned, leaden-blue fish, which clings tightly to objects by a sucking-disc on its belly.

Doris enters with a watering can

Doris I'll give the window-box a little drinkie while I'm at it.

Doris goes and is heard ascending the stairs

Marge While she's at what?

Lottie The window. She doesn't believe the house is being watched. How come you know all about lumpfish?

Marge "Fish Cookery for the Ambitious". Tolpuddle Evening Institute, Spring, nineteen seventy-nine. Did Doris pop into Oxfam?

Lottie I told her not to bother.

Marge But, Lottie, I need some new shoes!

Lottie Nonsense, Marge: you've a cupboard-full!

Marge They're dancing pumps, and at least thirty years old. They go back to the days when Roger and I were members of Iris Willis's Latin American Formation Team.

Lottie We're on the breadline, dear, and things are not going to improve. Not in this age of acquisition and greed. No-one would bat an eyelid were everyone over sixty-five to lie down, take a good swig of hemlock, and make a nice tidy end to things!

Marge Death didn't make a nice tidy end to things for poor Violet, did it?

Lottie Don't be morbid.

Marge Not even a Christian burial. I often wonder what they did with the body——

Lottie Just thank your lucky stars they weren't able to trace it to us!

Pause

Doris has been on the razzle, already. She's probably up there at this very minute, helping herself to another "little drinkie" along with her geraniums!

Marge Where does she get the money from?

Lottie Heaven knows! God knows I keep a very careful check on her! But, more puzzling still … where does she hide the booze? I've taken her room apart——

Marge (*appalled*) You've searched her room?

Lottie Our constitution clearly states there shall be no locked doors.

Pause

Her drinking's becoming a problem.

Marge It's nothing to what it used to be.

Lottie It was different when she lived alone, and before Violet.

Pause

Haven't you noticed the frequency with which she nips up to the loo during the evenings? Loo, be damned! She pops up to her room for a quick swig, and comes down on a pink cloud of peppermint and euphoria. Excuse me a moment, while I jot that down… (*She gets her notebook and writes in it*) "Vanda Lane … wafted down on a … pink cloud…"

Marge There are times I envy that Vanda Lane.

Lottie (*reading as she writes*) "…cloud of peppermint and euphoria … her delicate fingers … entwined about a refreshing *crème de menthe frappé*…"

Marge She never drops a vanilla ice-cream down the front of a brand new skirt…

Lottie (*reading as she writes*) "…served in a glittering crystal goblet…"

Marge Or misses the last bus, or mislays her teeth. She's got it made, what with being accident free, and endowed with high firm breasts, and thighs like polished alabaster.

Lottie Doesn't it occur to you that Doris is putting us all at risk? At the moment, it's the odd one on the way back from the shops; the next thing, it'll be two, then three. How long before she's chewing the fat with some of her old cronies, and becoming ... expansive ... should the subject of Violet ever crop up?

Marge She's not that much of a fool!

Lottie In her cups, she's every kind of a fool! How long before the fuzz carts us all off to the nearest nick?

Doris enters

Well? Is the girl still there?

Doris (*nodding*) She's taking notes.

Lottie There! Trouble! I knew it!

Marge I wonder what she wants.

Doris Go and ask her.

Marge Why me?

Lottie Well, you did take judo lessons at the Tolpuddle.

Marge Karate, but I never completed the course. It was interfering with my flamenco lessons. You go, Lottie: you're the one who knows the right sort of stories to tell, if she's from the DSS. Would you say she looked like a policeperson?

Doris She's wearing jeans, and an anorak.

Lottie Well, if she is casing the joint she'd hardly want to look like the fuzz, were she acting as a "tail", would she?

Marge I don't know what we're worrying about. We covered all our tracks, didn't we?

Lottie Unless you left a clear footprint, and they've been able to trace a thirty year old dancing pump back to us.

The doorbell rings. A slight pause as they look at each other

Who's going to answer it?

Doris Don't look at me: I'm the shortest.

Lottie But by far the heaviest.

Doris Marge is the one with pugilistic ambitions.

Marge I couldn't even toss a wineglass over my shoulder this morning.

Lottie (*taking the revolver from the drawer*) Both of you go; I'll stay here and give you back-up.

Marge and Doris go into the hall

Lottie stands behind the door. The front door is opened, and a mumble of voices heard

The door is closed, and Doris enters, followed by Ronnie, a sturdy girl of twenty, then Marge. Ronnie has an Australian accent

Lottie takes up an American police stance, legs apart, revolver held before her in both hands

Freeze!

Ronnie (*to Doris*) Is that gun for real?

Doris A war souvenir. (*She takes the gun from Lottie*) This is Violet's granddaughter, Ronnie.

Lottie What are you doing out of Australia?

Ronnie Oh, we're allowed out now, you know; it's no longer a penal colony.

Lottie Why were you taking notes?

Ronnie (*puzzled*) Notes? (*After a pause she laughs*) I was writing a couple of postcards: to folks back home.

Marge She's come to see her granny.

Lottie Violet wouldn't like that at all.

Ronnie Mum didn't ask me to come; she doesn't give a damn whether Gran's alive or dead.

Lottie Violet'd hate to be called Granny.

Ronnie Why? We all have to grow old, don't we? It's the natural order of things. Where is she?

Slight pause

Marge (*inspired*) On holiday.

Ronnie Where?

Marge Where did she say, Lottie?

Lottie Doris remembers, don't you, dear?

Doris Er—we don't know exactly.

Ronnie That's a bit weird, isn't it?

Doris Not really. It's a … a caravan holiday!

Ronnie At her age?

Marge Oh, she's still able to cock her leg high enough to get into the trailer.

Lottie Despite the natural order of things. Ronnie's an unusual name for a young girl, isn't it?

Ronnie I'm twenty, and it's short for Veronica.

Doris Oops! Must rush to the loo!

Doris exits

Ronnie When are you expecting Gran back?

Lottie (*looking at her exercise book*) How long are you here for?

Ronnie I go back on Wednesday.
Lottie Oh, what rotten luck. Isn't that rotten luck, Marge?
Marge Very rotten luck: she comes back on Thursday.
Lottie Why did you want to see her?
Ronnie I've always felt that anyone who hates Mum as much as she does can't be at all bad!
Lottie It's not so much hate, as the wish your mother had been born to someone else.
Ronnie Besides, I've always felt it unfair that other kids had two grans, but I never had one.
Marge It's time I got back to my cooking.

Marge goes into the kitchen and closes the door

Ronnie Did I say something?
Lottie Duty calls: she's our gastronomic genius. Give her a pound of herrings and a couple of crusty loaves, and she'll feed the entire borough. I'd offer you a cup of tea, had I the strength to overpower her, and take command of the kitchen.
Ronnie I had one just before I came.
Lottie Just as well. It would probably have been a re-cycled Earl Grey tea-bag. Marge got 'em cheap at a jumble sale, and they're absolutely disgusting!
Ronnie Then why don't you just throw them away?
Lottie Ah, but you see, by saving a few pennies on food, buying our clothes at jumble sales, cutting each other's hair, and not switching on electric fires until the temperature drops below freezing, we can have a week's holiday each year at Bexhill-on-Sea.
Ronnie Sounds great!
Lottie Off-season, half-board, at *Bella Vista*, just behind the bus station.
Ronnie Wonderful!
Lottie You can take my place any time. But the others seem to enjoy it. I gather you're none too fond of your mother?
Ronnie Hate her guts. It's mutual. Why has Gran——?
Lottie Violet.
Ronnie Why has Violet ignored Mum for all these years?
Lottie It was all to do with your father.
Ronnie My real father?
Lottie There can only be *one* father.
Ronnie Well, I've a stepfather, too, you know. Mum says my real dad died when I was three months old, trying to save a small boy from drowning. Why are you smiling? It's not true, is it? You don't have to lie to save my feelings, you know.

Pause

Lottie Your mother was the one whose father died when she was three
months old. Not you. During the war.
Ronnie Killed in action?
Lottie It might be construed that way, I suppose. He fell off a ladder, hanging
the holly in the canteen. Violet always said she'd have made a truly
beautiful widow, but, being wartime, decent black was very hard to come
by. She had to dye her wedding dress for the funeral.
Ronnie Didn't she marry again?
Lottie No, but she gave ... brief harbour ... to many ships that passed...

The kitchen door opens, and Marge pokes out her head

Marge Have you seen my pastry brush?
Lottie Last I saw of it, Doris had it.
Marge She'll have to go!

Marge slams the kitchen door shut

Ronnie What has Grandad's death got to do with my father?

Pause

Lottie Your mother, from all accounts, was an extremely ugly child——
Ronnie She's now an extremely ugly woman!
Lottie —completely bypassing the beauty and charm of her mother.
Ronnie Was Violet so beautiful and charming?
Lottie Ravishing, according to Violet. Anyway, there was your mother, first,
in her teens, then in her twenties, living the life of a geriatric nun, while
Violet was living the life of Old Riley! And, as it became distressingly clear
that your mother Gloria was not going to blossom into a swan, jealousy
set in.
Ronnie I still don't see where my father comes in.
Lottie Stage left, child, at this very moment. He was an Australian named
Bluey, who rode a monocycle in a travelling circus.
Ronnie Was it a big romance?
Lottie A brief encounter. He was old enough to be her father, which wasn't
surprising, considering he was Violet's current inamorato.
Ronnie And he seduced her daughter?
Lottie According to Violet, your mother caught poor Bluey, quite literally,
with his trousers down, answering the call of nature, and absolutely legless
with the drink. Your mother, it seems, never one for missing an opportu-

nity, crept up on him and pounced. Bluey swore it was over so quickly, she
might have been a passing shadow.

Marge emerges from the kitchen

Marge I'm off to class.
Lottie (*continuing her tale*) But for Gloria, it was a triumph! She'd usurped
her mother's bed!
Marge Well, if one's a stickler for accuracy, it was up against the side wall
of *The Knave of Hearts*. When you hear the pinger in the kitchen, will you
take the pie out of the oven to cool? And, should you chance upon Doris
trying to gain entry to the kitchen, shoot her dead!

Marge goes into the hall

Ronnie (*whispering*) What sort of class?
Lottie Swimming.
Ronnie At her age?
Lottie Will you please desist from referring to old age as if it were some
dreadful disease picked up from a lavatory seat?

Marge enters

Marge One of my gloves is missing. Oh well, I'll just have to keep one hand
in my pocket. Don't forget about the pie.
Lottie When the pinger——
Marge And don't forget about Doris: straight between the eyes!

Marge goes. The front door slams

Lottie Some day she'll have that door off its hinges.
Ronnie Did Bluey marry Mum?
Lottie Like some people offer a cup of tea, so he'd offer his hand in marriage.
Ronnie Bigamy?
Lottie On a truly heroic scale.

Pause

Ronnie So I'm a bastard?
Lottie A one-parent-something-or-other, to use the current euphemism. It
used to be "born on the wrong side of the blanket". But it all amounts to
the same thing: yes, child: you are a bastard.

Ronnie laughs

Oh, dear. I do hope that's not the prelude to a bout of hysterics.

Ronnie *(still laughing)* I love you, Lottie! I think it's great: the most marvellous thing that's ever happened to me. It makes me feel sort of ... special. Bluey sounds just the sort of a father I'd have invented for myself. Was he very handsome?

Lottie Like a Greek god, according to Violet. But then, of course, she *was* always prone to vast exaggeration.

Ronnie Are there no photographs of him?

Pause

Lottie Oh, I'm sure there must be one or two somewhere among her things...

Ronnie *(excitedly)* Do look! Please! It's like ... being born all over again!

Lottie Very well. I'll go up and see what I can find. If you like you can have a peek at my novel. It has a ... cheeky little presumption which I think you'll find amusing.

Lottie goes, and quickly ascends the stairs

Ronnie begins reading the book. A moment later much slower steps are heard descending the stairs

Doris enters. She has been drinking

Doris What's she doing in Violet's room?

Ronnie Looking for some old photographs.

Doris Did she tell you you could read that?

Ronnie Yes.

Doris Load of old crap, isn't it? But we all have our little foibles, don't we? Apart from seeing herself as England's answer to Raymond Chandler, Lottie's main one is a totally unfounded conviction that the co-operative is the perfect way of life.

Ronnie Well, I'd say it has a lot going for it, if people who need each other get toget——

Doris It's like a prison. Lottie could live in a vacuum. But not me: nor Marge. I mean, if Marge lived in a vacuum, where would she keep all her junk?

Ronnie What junk?

Doris Her foible's an enquiring mind. For years, now, she's had the entire staff at the Evening Institute run off its feet while she's journeyed into the mysteries of the contrabassoon, karate, trade-unionism, creative cookery, dried flower arrangement, archery, furniture restoration, and Spanish dancing: to name but a few. The relics of which reside in her room like the debris from some gargantuan orgy. Where is she, by the way?

Ronnie Swimming.
Doris Ah, yes. Flavour of the month. I suspect that means we'll have her
prancing about the beach at Bexhill in a bikini next year.
Ronnie I thought Bexhill was a special treat?
Doris For who? We go because it doesn't cost much, and it doesn't cost much
because you don't get much. But the other two seem to enjoy it… (*She
shrugs*)

Slight pause

Ronnie And what's your foible?
Doris Drink.
Ronnie Just … drink?
Doris Well, it has to be alcoholic, of course. Port and lemon, or rum and
blackcurrant, for choice. But I'm not fussy. Anything, really. Not that the
community chest allows money for that sort of thing. Oh, no!

Slight pause

(*In a conspiratorial whisper*) In fact, the co-op's made a sort of … criminal
of me.
Ronnie In what way?
Doris (*loud whisper*) I've had to devise a … secret … dishonest means of
… stashing away enough dosh … for the odd tipple now and then…

Pause

Ronnie You just said "the other two" enjoy Bexhill…
Doris Did I? Well, I've had one or two little tots this morning….
Ronnie (*thoughtfully*) And a little while ago, when Lottie was talking about
Violet, she said Violet *was* always prone to exaggeration. Past tense: as if
she wasn't … coming back.
Doris (*nervous laugh*) Oh, you know what writers are like. No respect for
grammar. Make it up as they go along; "style" they call it. (*After a slight
pause she deliberately changes the subject, her tone a little too bright*)
What were you talking about while I was upstairs?
Ronnie My father.
Doris And Violet?
Ronnie And Violet.
Doris That must have been nice for you. I do hope she's having a nice time
down in … in … wherever Marge said she'd gone to.
Ronnie Are you sure there isn't something else I should know? About Gran,
that is?

Doris (*too brightly*) What a suspicious girl you are! What could there
possibly be?

Ronnie (*doubtfully*) I don't know. (*After a slight pause she, too, is a little too
bright*) Talking of drink's given me a thirst. (*She laughs*) It's thirsty work,
I can tell you, suddenly being told you're a bastard!

Doris Eh?

Ronnie I'm a bastard: isn't it great?

Doris Are you sure you've not already been drinking?

Ronnie What d'you say? Why don't we go out and celebrate? Just the two
of us. After all, it's not every day you get a visitor from down under! Let's
go along the road for a couple of drinkies.

Doris (*tempted*) Well... I wouldn't be able to buy you one...

Ronnie Ronnie's treat.

Doris Just so long as that's understood.

Ronnie I've a couple of cards to post, anyway.

Doris Then what are we waiting for? But we'd better creep out softly. Lottie
doesn't approve of my drinking...

Ronnie (*whispering*) We'll be as quiet as mice...

*Doris giggles as they creep into the hall. A moment later the front door is
quietly closed*

*Shortly, Lottie's footsteps descend the stairs, and she enters the room
looking at a couple of black and white photographs*

Lottie I'm sorry I took so long, but... (*She stops, surprised, at seeing the
room empty*)

Lottie looks into the kitchen, then goes into the hall

(*Off; calling*) Doris! Doris!

*Lottie is heard climbing the stairs and opening a door. A moment later she
rushes down the stairs and into the living-room. She pauses, deciding what
to do, then goes into the hall and a moment later the front door is heard to
close*

The pinger sounds in the kitchen. The stage darkens

SCENE 2

One hour later

Lottie sits working at her novel, pausing occasionally, her mind wandering. The front door opens and closes and she turns, expectantly

Marge enters

Lottie Oh, it's you.
Marge (*taking off her coat*) Sorry: maybe I should go back and drown? (*She sniffs the air*)
Lottie Yes, it's sad news, I'm afraid.
Marge The pie!

Marge throws down her coat and rushes into the kitchen

Lottie I'm truly sorry, dear; it's a sort of … dark mahogany colour.

Marge enters crestfallen

Marge That pinger can be heard from Land's End to John O'Groats!
Lottie I wasn't here——
Marge Next time I'm passing Oxfam I'll see if I can get you an ear-trumpet!

Marge removes her hat, takes it into the hall together with her coat, and re-enters

Lottie Doris is missing.
Marge Since the place smells like a forest fire, who can blame her? She probably fled to safety, with her hair smouldering!
Lottie This is serious.
Marge I'll say it is. I spent all morning on that pie. I suppose you were far too engrossed in the exploits of the lovely Vanda, stuffing keys, half-eaten apples, and the like, down that desirable bosom of hers?
Lottie I was out, trying to trace Doris—she's on the loose!
Marge What sort of a state was she in?
Lottie I didn't see her go.
Marge I'll rephrase the question: what sort of a state were you in?
Lottie I went upstairs to fetch some photographs, and when I came down, they were both gone. Together, I feel sure.
Marge But … why?
Lottie I'd have thought it obvious. The girl's taken her out to find out what she can about Violet.

Marge You think she didn't believe our caravan saga?
Lottie Who knows what doubts Doris has put into her head. I rushed out and looked in all of the awful spit-and-sawdust saloons she used to frequent. But there was no sign of them.

Pause

She's dangerous, if she spills the beans. They both are.
Marge Even if she does, what can we do?
Lottie As you said earlier, she'll have to go.
Marge Go? Where?
Lottie We'll decide when we know the damage.

Pause

Marge D'you think she will rat on us?
Lottie A few drinks and she'll sing like a canary. As Tod once remarked, in a moment of brute philosophy, "You show me a crooked broad who's a lush, and I'll show you one twenty-two-carat stool-pigeon!"

Pause

Marge Doris isn't exactly "a crooked broad," is she? Nor are we planning for her to end up at the bottom of some river, wearing a concrete overcoat. I mean, who'd help us carry a bath of cement, plus Doris, up the Putney towpath?
Lottie Be serious!
Marge I'm trying awfully hard, but the conversation appears to have got … a little bit out of hand. What, precisely, have you in mind for her?
Lottie Well, it would certainly need to be … something pretty drastic!
Marge Dare I ask … how drastic?

The doorbell rings

Well, it's not Doris: she has a key.
Lottie (*on her way to the door*) "But," I ask myself, "is she able to locate the keyhole?"

Lottie goes into the hall and returns with Ronnie

Marge Where's Doris?
Ronnie Sleeping: on a bench by the cemetery.
Marge Oh, dear. (*To Lottie*) Shall I take Big Bella and pick her up?

Ronnie "Big Bella"?

Marge The old banger.

Lottie The car. Our only luxury. Something one of Marge's husbands left when he went in search of better things. (*To Marge*) You'd better, dear. I'd rather she was here, where we can keep an eye on her.

Marge puts on her coat and exits

Pause

Ronnie Doris'd knocked back a good few before we went out.

Lottie Oh, but I feel sure she served her purpose before blacking out.

Ronnie (*innocently*) Purpose?

Lottie Information.

Ronnie Oh, that.

Lottie Yes. That.

Ronnie About Violet being dead? Why shouldn't I know? I'm one of the family.

Lottie Only by default. How much did she tell you?

Ronnie She went on about poor Violet not having had a Christian burial, and about her poor body having been dumped in a railway siding in the back of beyond.

Lottie She wasn't dumped: she was placed very lovingly on a slab, in an extremely well-kept graveyard, hovered over by a sexually ambiguous angel which had two fingers and half its nose missing, but an expression on its face of deep concern. As for being in the back of beyond, she was on a route with at least three buses into the town centre!

Ronnie But ... why do that to her?

Lottie Well ... this is a rented house, with Violet's name on the rent book... Just out of curiosity, which pub did Doris take you to?

Ronnie *The Knave of Hearts.* She showed me the bit of wall where I was thought to have been conceived: she felt it was the next best thing to having known my father.

Lottie Violet was mugged: on a dark December afternoon.

Ronnie On the doorstep, Doris said.

Lottie That's where we found her.

Ronnie Did nobody see it?

Lottie No. The neighbours were having their monthly crime-watch meeting.

Ronnie And she refused to see the doctor?

Lottie She said to get one in the morning, if she felt no better. She felt nothing by then, of course. She was dead.

Ronnie Heart?

Lottie It'd stopped beating, if that's what's worrying you.

Ronnie It must have been an awful shock.

Lottie Oh, it was: she wasn't insured.

Ronnie So that's why you dumped the body?

Lottie Will you please get it into your head, child, that we did not dump the body. We simply had more to think about than mere formalities, like funerals. Had we publicly announced she'd died, we'd have found ourselves on the pavement before you could say RIP! The landlord's wanted her out for years. He has grandiose schemes for converting this place into a couple of self-contained furnished luxury flatlets which would fetch him twenty times what we pay. Besides, we'd also have had to give up her pension book, which is a vital part of our economy.

Pause

We decided to drive north.

Ronnie Eh?

Lottie For the final resting place.

Ronnie Why north?

Lottie Big Bella was aimed in that direction, and Marge's three-point turn is sure-fire invitation to disaster.

Ronnie What did you do with Violet? Bundle her into the boot?

Lottie She sat in the back seat next to Doris, who consumed a complete bottle of port during the trip.

Ronnie Doesn't it disturb you, not knowing what they did with the body when they found it?

Lottie No. We've agreed that when any of us die, the others take her to some green and pleasant spot, and leave her there.

Ronnie If everyone did that, the countryside would be knee-deep in dead little old ladies.

Lottie But everyone won't do that, will they? They'll go on preferring seeing their loved ones off with pomp and ceremony. We feel it's better to spend the money on the living.

Ronnie Well, it's certainly an original viewpoint. How did you all come to be here, together, in the one house?

Lottie Well, as I said, it was Violet's house; she'd been here since the war, when she was married. Marge, Doris and I each had a bed-sitter. Poky little rooms, with gas rings, and beds that sagged in the middle. We all used to meet in the library, where it was warm ... being ladies of slender means, you understand...?

Pause

Whatever happened to that "fruitful old age" we're all supposed to be enjoying? "Frightful old age" is nearer the truth. Poor Marge hadn't had a holiday for over seven years, and Doris found staying drunk helped shut out the awfulness of her room. Mine wasn't much better. Anyway, we'd sit toasting our toes by the library radiator, discussing the merits of a joint effort, and then, one day ... decided it was time to get ourselves sorted out. Which we did. Well, more or less. As you can see, Doris has had a relapse.

A key is heard in the front door

Speak of the devil...

The door opens, then closes. Sluggish footsteps ascend the stairs

Marge enters, taking off her coat, which she then hangs in the hall

Marge She's gone up to sleep it off.

Pause

Well? Did she spill the beans?
Lottie Oh, she squealed all right!

Pause

Marge So where does that leave us?
Lottie Facing a murder rap, if we're not careful.
Ronnie Murder?
Lottie The pathologist's report showed she'd died from several blows to the head.
Marge With a blunt instrument; it was in the newspapers.
Lottie And under suspicious circumstances: all the labels on her clothing had been removed.
Marge To confuse the police, you know. It's what I felt Tod Mallett would have done.
Lottie A waste of time, really. Mainly Marks and Sparks, and British Home Stores. But it was good thinking, Marge!

Pause

Marge And what do you intend doing with your hard-earned knowledge?
Ronnie I was just curious...
Lottie That doesn't really answer Marge's question, does it?

Pause

Ronnie All right, then: I think I'd like to join your co-operative, please, if I
   may.
Lottie No, you may not. I thought you were returning to Australia?
Ronnie Changing her mind is a woman's prerogative.
Marge Why have you changed your mind?
Ronnie Well ... you're hardly going to believe this ... but ... well... I feel
   really at home here.
Marge In this house?
Ronnie I've never considered it home over there. Not a real home. But, this
   ... wow!
Lottie Wow, indeed!
Ronnie I've never considered myself part of ... a family. Oh, it was fine for
   the other kids——
Lottie What other kids?
Ronnie Mum had two by my stepfather.
Marge I expect there's little other entertainment in the outback.
Ronnie Ray and Debbie. He made a great big fuss of them, but was always
   very cool to me; I thought it was just because he wasn't my real dad. (*After
   a pause she laughs*) Oh, to hell with the lot of 'em! Well? Am I to become
   a fully-paid-up member of Hell's Angels?

Pause

Lottie We haven't the space.
Ronnie What about Violet's room?
Lottie We sold her bed.
Marge I'm sure it found a good home.

Pause

Ronnie (*slyly*) You don't think it more ... sensible ... for all the people who
   know about this to be under one roof? To ... sort of ... keep an eye on each
   other, if you see what I mean?
Lottie I'm way ahead of you, child. You mean ... lest someone else should
   decide to ... unbutton her lip?
Ronnie Oh, not with malice aforethought. *In vino veritas*, perhaps?

Pause

Lottie Blackmail!
Marge Said Tod Mallett, a hint of menace troubling his coal-black eyes!
Ronnie More ... an insurance policy, I'd have said. Of course, I realize the
   risk I'd be taking...

Marge What risk?

Ronnie Well, I've only your word for it that she was mugged by a passing stranger. How do I know one of you didn't bump her off?

Lottie Why should we want to bump off poor old Violet?

Ronnie The house? Her pension book? Maybe she had a fortune stashed away under her mattress?

Lottie If one of us really had killed her, you——

Ronnie Maybe you all had a hand in it. Isn't that what a co-operative's all about?

Lottie It's not a euphemism for Murder Incorporated. But, I take your point, child: we could have killed her, and have no way of proving otherwise.

Marge But nor has she!

Lottie True, but we don't want to rock the boat, do we?

Marge (*vehemently*) I could kill Doris!

Lottie I think it only fair we draw lots for that privilege!

Pause

Very well, child: you can have the put-u-up in the downstairs front room.

Marge Directly on to the traffic.

Ronnie Sounds great!

Marge The springs are like a rare medieval torture!

Lottie Oh, I think Ronnie's hide is thick enough to shrug off a few springs.

Ronnie You'll not regret this.

Lottie Let's hope you don't. (*She stands*) If one, or all of us, really did kill Violet, could you ever feel safe enough to get a good night's sleep while you're in this house? The room's this way.

Lottie smiles, and leads Ronnie off, as Marge watches them go

The stage darkens

SCENE 3

The following Thursday. Morning

Lottie reads aloud from her novel, while Marge wrestles with a complicated Fair Isle pattern. The doors to both the kitchen and the garden are open

Lottie (*reading*) "Chapter Nine. 'She was a stoolie,' Tod said, turning his dark, moody eyes on Vanda, 'and there's no room on life's carousel for a stoolie.' 'I guess you're right, boss,' Vanda valiantly volunteered——'"

Marge She—WHAT!?
Lottie (*firmly*) Valiantly volunteered! (*She continues reading*) "'But whenever I see a broad with a hole where the back of her head used to be, I can't help asking myself, 'Was she somebody's mother?' Tod grinned a rugged boyish grin. 'Save your finer feelings for some other ball-game, kiddo: stoolies is nothing but nature's trash!'"
Marge (*mumbling*) ...knit two together at the end of alternate rows... (*After a pause she looks up*) Do you see Doris as a stoolie?
Lottie Don't you?
Marge I can't see her as part of nature's trash.
Lottie She blew the whistle on us, didn't she?

Pause

Marge Nor do I think she merits a grisly end. (*After a pause she holds out her knitting for Lottie to inspect*) What does that look like to you?
Lottie (*slight deliberation*) An ... elephant?
Marge Oh, dear, it's supposed to be a camel. Of course, dear Roger was always better at this sort of thing.
Lottie Your first husband?
Marge Will you never learn? The second. Alan was the first, may he rest in peace. But at least he died in a moment of supreme ecstasy.
Lottie In bed?
Marge In the amphitheatre, at Covent Garden, applauding Callas's *Tosca*. At least, he began in the amphitheatre, but foolishly stood on his seat, lost his balance, and was hurled into the stalls at a frightening pace. Maria was furious, of course, finding herself upstaged during her moment of triumph. (*She surveys her knitting*) This strange-looking camel thing is ... I think ... a dropped stitch that's ... sort of run.
Lottie This business of Doris is serious. She tried creeping out again last night. Ronnie saw her.
Marge Now there's someone I trust no farther than I can throw a grand piano!
Lottie Be fair, dear, you've known her less than a week. The combination of Doris and the bottle——
Marge Are you, by any chance, fantasizing a situation wherein you bump her off, and drop her into the Thames wearing a concrete overcoat? Personally, I'd as soon that sort of thing happened to Waltzing Matilda.
Lottie Ronnie's a godsend. That refund on her air ticket could well mean a few extra days at Bexhill next spring! Besides, it's time we had some new blood.
Marge I suppose we should convene a meeting, really, and discuss the thing properly.
Lottie You're quite right, dear. (*She opens a drawer, takes out a minutes book, and opens it*) There! I declare this meeting open.

Marge (*surprised*) Just like that?
Lottie You've something better to do?
Marge Well ... no...
Lottie Good, then that's carried.
Marge Damn! I can't remember whether this is the alternative row, or not.
Lottie Oh, for heaven's sake, put the wretched thing down and concentrate!

Marge savagely thrusts the needles into the ball of wool, and throws it on to the sideboard

That's the spirit! The thrust of those pins would have done a matador proud!
Marge I'd like it placed on record that under no circumstances am I stabbing Doris to death with a number eleven knitting needle! Shouldn't she be here?
Lottie We can hardly discuss her fate, with her sat across the table, can we?
Marge Then what about Waltzing Matilda?
Lottie She's busy, doing community work: it would be a pity to disturb her.
Marge What if we disagree on a motion?
Lottie No problem: I have the casting vote.
Marge Why you?
Lottie Chairperson.
Marge You were chairperson last time.
Lottie I stood in for Doris, who was incapable of standing at all. This is my official turn.
Marge It seems very undemocratic to me.
Lottie Very well, I'll get Ronnie.
Marge What's she doing, anyway?
Lottie Clearing out the garden shed, to get at the mower; she's going to cut the lawn. And we're to grow vegetables.
Marge Gardening? With our backs?
Lottie She's promised to do the manual labour.
Marge Developing into quite the little Jill of all trades, isn't she? Doesn't, by any freak chance, happen to dance the lead in *Swan Lake* at Covent Garden on her night off?
Lottie It's time that shed was cleared.
Marge Must be one heaving mass of spiders. Not that it's the spiders, themselves, that give me the creeps, just the legs. Eight seems to give them such an unfair advantage when it comes to running. Should present no problem for her, though. Down under, they have them the size of dinner plates, apparently.
Lottie I'll go and fetch Ronnie.

Lottie goes through the kitchen and into the garden

Doris pokes her head round the door from the hall

Doris (*whispering*) I've been listening at the top of the stairs.

Marge Oh, hallo, Doris.

Doris Sitting up in my room alone's driving me round the twist. They act as if I'm not here. I'm well and truly in the doghouse, aren't I? I've apologized for last Saturday.

Marge Insufficient, dear: melodrama was on the cards. Hara-kiri, at the very least.

Doris I was led on.

Marge With cold calculation.

Doris Deliberately indulged.

Marge Unmercifully.

Doris Then why's Lottie so cold? And so friendly with ... her?

Marge Minds with but a single thought. I suspect the co-operative's about to be restructured on a more militant basis. Wouldn't be surprised if they had us in uniforms before the month's out. Ronnie said she caught you trying to sneak out last night.

Doris It's a lie! I swear it! I mean, where would I be going?

Marge Well, in order of distance, there's *The Prodigal Son*, to start with——

Doris D'you think Reg and Maize are fool enough to let me drink on credit?

Marge You've usually had the odd shilling up the leg of your bloomers.

Doris Ah, but that was when I was allowed to do the shopping.

Marge So you were fiddling the books! Clever old you! You had Lottie fooled.

Doris But why should Ronnie lie about me? (*After a pause she sighs*) I don't know why I ever got myself involved with this set-up. I must have been drunk!

Marge Come to think of it——

Doris I'm not really cut out for regimentation. I'm more of a free spirit. There are times I dream of the sheer pleasure of lying in a ditch ... absolutely pissed out of my tiny mind!

Marge Oh, not a ditch, dear: ditches are only for nature's trash.

Doris (*dreamily*) Or eating out of tins ... or munching a Big Mac and french fries...

Marge If my cooking's not good——

Doris No offence, love. You do your best with what you're allocated, but a packet of dried peas and a bag of flour don't exactly add up to *cordon bleu*, do they?

Marge Come now, Doris, life's not that bad. We all have our impossible dreams.

Doris (*interested*) Oh? What's your dream, then?

Marge Shoes! New shoes! To go into a shoe emporium ... preferably
something terribly chic, in Bond Street ... and, without having to look at
the price tag, choose any pair that took my fancy. To browse ... trying on
everything in the shop! And then to teeter along the pavement in six inch
heels, like some outrageously expensive tart! (*She sighs, and resumes her
knitting*)

Doris At your age, they'd cripple you!

Marge (*laughing*) You're probably right. Ah well, as the intrepid Tod
Mallett would no doubt tell us: "Walking on spikes is no occupation for an
ageing doll!"

Pause

Doris Nor is walking a tightrope. I've reached a point where I'm afraid to
open my mouth.

Pause

And another thing ... nothing personal ... but these holidays down at
Bexhill ... frankly, Marge, they get on my tits!

Marge Mine, too, dear.

Doris I'd rather scrub floors.

Marge Latrines.

Doris ⎱
Marge ⎰ (*together*) With a toothbrush!

They laugh

Doris Then why do we go?

Marge To see the look of rapture on Lottie's face, I suppose.

Doris D'you think she has an impossible dream?

Marge (*idly*) To win the Pulitzer prize for literature, perhaps?

Doris With that crap?

Marge Every beetle is a gazelle in the eyes of its mother.

Pause

*Lottie enters the kitchen, unseen by Doris and Marge, and puts the
kettle on*

Doris I've a good mind to take my pension book and go.

Lottie pauses to listen

Marge Where?
Doris I don't know.

Pause

Moira's going to have a spare room, once Paddy's funeral's over. I
could——
Lottie (*off; brightly*) Ah, you're up, then, Doris? I'm just making a nice cup
of tea.

Lottie enters from the kitchen and takes a close look at Marge's knitting

Of course that's a camel, Marge. I must have been mad to think otherwise.
Marge What happened to Waltzing Matilda.
Lottie She prefers to finish what she's doing. What about a nice garibaldi
with our tea?

Lottie goes into the kitchen and rummages around

(*Off*) They're here, somewhere.
Doris (*whispering*) What's come over her?
Marge (*whispering*) I don't know: but I don't much like it. There's dirty
work at the crossroads.
Doris (*loudly*) What *is* Ronnie doing?
Lottie (*off*) Clearing the shed. You'd be surprised at what's in there.
Marge I think I'd rather not know.

Lottie enters

Lottie What you were saying earlier, Marge... You know, about getting rid
of her...
Doris (*eagerly*) Getting rid of her?
Marge It's not quite what you think——
Doris How soon?
Lottie You see... I've been giving the matter some serious thought...
Doris Of course, it would mean buying her another return ticket...
Marge Oh, she won't need a ticket for the place Lottie has in mind.
Doris (*puzzled*) Where's that?
Lottie She's a threat, Doris: surely you can see that?
Doris (*doggedly*) Where?
Lottie (*brightly*) Well, where we left poor Violet, if Marge thinks she can
find the spot again. They'd be sort of ... company for each other, if you
see——

Doris You mean ... dead?
Lottie (*equally brightly*) As a door-nail, dear.

The whistling kettle sounds

Lottie goes into the kitchen

(*Off*) If you don't care for a garibaldi, I think we've still a custard cream or two. Now, whatever you do, Doris, you mustn't feel guilty about Ronnie——
Doris *Me* feel guilty? You're the one——
Lottie (*off*) After all, you're the one who blabbed.
Doris (*softly*) It's a joke, isn't it?
Marge I've a gut feeling it's not.
Lottie (*off*) When our very mode of existence is threatened——
Doris Threatened or not, I will not be a party to ... cold-blooded murder!

Lottie enters with a tray containing cups, etc.

Lottie And there's a slice of lemon from the weekend, for anyone who prefers to go Russian. It's an execution, Doris. Justifiable homicide.
Doris You've been taking that silly book of yours too seriously.
Lottie If you are referring to *Baby, Here's Your Shroud*——
Doris She's inhuman, that ... monster with the alabaster thighs!
Lottie It's not as if you're being asked to actually ... perform ... but simply to ... be there. Purely a question of joint responsibility. One for all, and all for one. Like the three musketeers.
Doris We're four musketeers.
Lottie Only on the way up, if all goes well.
Marge And what if all doesn't go well?
Doris Like the gun not going off. I expect that's the ... *modus operandi* you've got in mind. Or what if you were to miss? You're no Annie Oakley, are you?

Lottie goes into the kitchen

Lottie (*off*) We'll just have to...

Lottie enters with the tea

...improvise.
Marge Do go on, it's getting interesting.
Lottie (*vaguely*) Well ... we could ... pop a few garden tools into the boot of the car...

Doris You mean, you're planning to bash her head in with a spade?
Lottie Well, I thought we might draw lots as to who actually does the deed, but that's a mere technicality. Yes; something along those lines.
Doris I'm sorry, Lottie, but dead bodies are just not my scene. Not even Ronnie's.

Pause

Lottie (*casually*) Of course ... you'd be ... well-fortified.

Pause

Doris How ... well-fortified?
Lottie A bottle of rum.
Doris A full bottle?
Lottie Oh, it's no time for doing things by halves.

Pause

Doris You couldn't see your way clear to throwing in a bottle of blackcurrant cordial, I suppose?
Lottie (*jovially*) Oh, let's go mad!
Doris It's certainly ... an attractive proposition.

Pause

Marge And what's my bribe to be?
Lottie Bribe? Really, Marge. Where's your loyalty to the cause?
Marge Full six fathoms deep in self-interest.
Lottie You don't really need a bribe, do you?
Marge Make me an offer I can't refuse.

Pause

Lottie What if the kitty were to provide the wherewithal for you to create a super-de-luxe gourmet dinner? (*Pointedly*) For three people.

Pause

Marge With smoked salmon and fillet steaks?
Lottie And *petit-fours* with the coffee.
Doris (*loud whisper*) Don't forget the wine, Marge. Lots and lots of lovely wine.

Marge Why do I get the feeling you're getting the best of all worlds?
Lottie (*heavily*) This dinner for three people being for tomorrow evening.
Marge Perhaps … to open on a sophisticated note … a couple of *crème de menthe frappés* …
Lottie Let us not over-reach our——
Marge If she whose breasts are the very pinnacles of ecstasy can drink them, I see no reason why possessors of bosoms more in need of a little … support … should be denied the same privilege.
Lottie (*resignedly*) *Crème de menthe frappés* it shall be. You realize, though, don't you, that means the … elimination … has to be done tonight.
Doris (*alarmed*) Does it?
Lottie Why prevaricate?
Marge Hamlet did, and we all know how messily that little domestic upset ended.
Doris I'd just like … time to prepare…
Marge (*thoughtfully*) Perhaps … for the meat course … a bottle of Mâcon Rouge … and for the sweet——
Lottie Cast your mind off your guts and pay attention. I just said——
Marge Tonight. So, who's arguing? How much petrol is there in the tank?
Doris You're as cold-blooded as she is!
Marge What would the police think, were we to break down miles from anywhere, with a Luger in the glove compartment, and the boot stuffed to the gills with offensive weapons?
Doris Garden tools?
Marge Highly offensive, if one's just struck a mortal blow and it's still sticky with the blood from the victim.
Doris I think I'm going to be sick.
Lottie She's right, Doris; I think we'd better check the tank.
Doris Shall I do it? I need a bit of air.
Lottie If you'd be so kind, dear.
Marge And please try not to be sick all over the driving seat: that's the one I'll be occupying.

Doris goes out through the hall

A slight pause. Marge resumes her knitting

Why the sudden change of heart?
Lottie (*innocently*) What's that, dear?
Marge Doling out goodies, like it was Christmas. And if that vacant expression's intended to suggest innocence, all it does is highlight the ravages of time. Twenty minutes ago you couldn't get Doris into a concrete overcoat fast enough. Now it's Waltzing Matilda for the high jump. I can't keep up with you: the situation's beginning to resemble Russian roulette.

Lottie You heard Doris: she's threatening to take her pension book and go, which would be a great blow to the economy.

Marge Ah, so you overheard?

Lottie Once she'd spilled the beans to Moira, it'd be tantamount to selling our story to the gutter press!

Pause

Marge (*quietly*) I'll have no hand in it.

Lottie But you said——

Marge Why shouldn't she drink? Heaven knows life's done her no favours. No, I'll have no hand in harming her.

Lottie But a moment ago you seemed quite agreeable——

Marge The other one, yes: not Doris.

Lottie You're simply not thinking it through.

Ronnie enters the kitchen

Marge hears her and changes the conversation

Marge Its food is not digested in the stomach but in the large, muscular two-part crop…

Ronnie comes into the room

(*Feigning surprise at seeing her*) Ah, the intrepid explorer returns!

Pause

Ronnie (*to Lottie*) Well?

Lottie Marge isn't convinced.

Marge Are we talking about Doris?

Ronnie She tried to get out again last night.

Marge So I'm told.

Ronnie Don't you believe me?

Marge Doris says she didn't.

Lottie Do you expect her to admit to it?

Marge (*slight pause*) I can understand that Doris might lie. What I fail to understand is why Ronnie should be so eager to see her dead.

Ronnie Not eager, Marge; I feel it's necessary, for the sake of you and Lottie.

Marge Come, dear: in my cynical experience altruism's usually no more than a domino mask. What's in it for you?

Pause

Ronnie I feel at home here, and a place that feels like home must be protected. (*She moves across to the hall, making an "exit"*) You see, I've never had a real home before; that's why it's so precious to me. Well, I'm going up to wash away the cobwebs; we'll talk about it some more when I come down.

Ronnie exits and is heard ascending the stairs

Marge Didn't your heart bleed for her as she lowered her eyelids and left?
Lottie (*thoughtfully*) That last speech had a … familiar ring to it.
Marge Given a swivel of pneumatic hips, and a quick flutter of six-inch eyelashes, it could have been Vanda talking.
Lottie (*urgently*) Hand me my novel, dear; I've a funny feeling it *was* Vanda talking.

Marge hands it to her. Lottie leafs through it

If you remember, her mother was pushed down a lift-shaft by a drug-crazed bell-hop——
Marge Nine floors, not counting the mezzanine——
Lottie —and her father was eaten by an alligator in the Everglades… (*More feverish searching*) … which is why she went to live on that crumbling old plantation way down in the Deep South…
Marge (*mumbling*) Knit to the end of the row, and then…
Lottie Where this strange woman used to make gestures to her from a window in the deserted east wing…
Marge …change to autumn russet, and purl three. Who turned out to be her Uncle Seth, a notorious transvestite, if my memory serves me correctly? Did you base him on my second husband?
Lottie Subconsciously, perhaps…
Marge Roger would have been flattered. He was fun: when he wasn't stretching my shoes or wearing my last decent pair of tights. Pity I couldn't keep him in the style of dress he aspired to.
Lottie Eureka! Here it is. (*She reads*) "Vanda turned to him, her lustrous eyes wider, her lips fuller and more desirable. Tod's heart pounded. 'You see, I've never had a real home before,' she whispered hoarsely, 'That's why it's so precious to me!'"

Pause

Well!

Pause

Of course, it could still be true that she's doing it for us.

Marge She's planning a take-over bid, if you want my opinion.

Pause

Lottie (*sighing*) You could be right. Doris is a bit of a problem, though.

Marge Look: who's to say I wouldn't turn stoolie for a week's gastronomic tour of Normandy? Or that you wouldn't, were some lunatic publisher to offer you a huge advance, and the printing of *Baby, Here's Your Shroud*? But that's all speculation: Ronnie's blackmail is hard fact! And, having got away with it once, who knows what her next demand will be. She presents far more danger, as far as I'm concerned. (*She counts the stitches on her knitting*) But we might as well get one thing clear. If it's Doris who's to bite the dust, count me out.

Lottie You're right, of course.

Marge So where does that leave us?

Lottie Ronnie it is!

Marge You mean that?

Lottie For the sake of the co-operative.

Marge Vive la co-operative! In that case, I'd better organize that dinner, hadn't I? Pity there's not to be a fourth. Someone to … fill up the other side of the table…

Lottie Operations begin at twenty-one hundred hours.

Marge Do we synchronize our watches?

Lottie Where's the point? Yours gains about five minutes to the hour.

Marge Oh, I've learned to compensate——

Lottie Don't bother, dear; I'll let you know when it's nine o'clock.

Marge (*getting up and moving toward the door*) Perhaps, instead of smoked salmon, I'll do leeks wrapped in Parma ham, with pear sauce…

Marge goes into the kitchen

A tiny smile appears on Lottie's face as she begins writing in her book. The stage darkens

SCENE 4

Seven thirty the following evening

Lottie is setting the table for four, stopping every now and then to jot down a few words in her book. Marge is in the kitchen, preparing the meal, from whence she conducts her part of the conversation, occasionally leaning

against the doorpost. Both are semi-formally dressed: Marge's outfit
something from her ballroom days

Lottie God! The way that rain came down! I was in half a mind to get you to turn back. There's nothing like a thunderstorm for dampening one's ardour, is there?

Marge (*off*) King Lear got quite turned on by 'em.

Lottie Was that him you were quoting last night?

Marge (*off*) At half past one this morning, to be exact.

Lottie Give or take an hour or two, your watch being what it is.

Marge (*off*) "Blow winds, and crack your cheeks! Rage! Blow!"

Lottie You looked like a madwoman.

Marge (*off*) Someone had to break the silence while you fumbled around, searching for the gun.

Lottie It'd got caught in the lining of my handbag. God! It was dramatic, wasn't it?

Marge (*off*) As dramatic as a Marx Brothers movie! Bang! "Oh, dear, I've missed her, haven't I?" Bang! "Did I hit her that time?" Bang! What are you writing? If you're quoting me, I'll speak more slowly.

Lottie I'm not.

Marge (*off*) Then what are you writing?

Lottie Great novels are based on true experience, and I don't want this incident to lose its ... flavour.

Marge (*off*) How did "great novels" worm their way into the conversation? I thought you knew how to fire that thing.

Lottie I'm surprised *you* never took evening classes for gun-craft, or whatever they call it. You seem to have taken classes for just about everything else.

Marge (*off*) Guns weren't on the curriculum: I had to make do with archery.

Lottie Maybe, next time, we'll make a bow and arrow our *modus operandi*.

Marge (*off*) Next time?

Lottie In a manner of speaking.

Marge (*off*) You're not planning murder as a cottage industry, by any chance?

The pinger sounds; Marge attends to the food

Lottie Would you like to hear what I've written?

Marge (*off*) I'd much rather hear about the fourth person who's coming to dinner.

Lottie So much tidier than a blank wall. Besides, we can play whist afterwards.

Marge (*off*) You loathe card games.

Lottie Only because I'm unlucky.
Marge (*off*) Nonsense! You're possibly the world's worst player, if you want the truth; and certainly the world's worst loser. Is it a friend of yours?
Lottie Who?
Marge (*off*) The dinner guest.
Lottie Well... I wouldn't go so far as to describe her as ... an actual friend.
Marge (*off*) How far, precisely, would you go ... if pushed?
Lottie An ... acquaintance.
Marge (*off*) How old an acquaintance?
Lottie In passing, so to speak.
Marge (*off*) How close in passing? Two feet? The other side of the road? The next borough?
Lottie By sight: if she's who I think she is. If she's that little woman with the awful dyed hair, orange lipstick, and bat sleeves, who I'm thinking of.
Marge (*off*) What little woman with the awful dyed hair, orange lipstick, and bat sleeves, who you're thinking of?
Lottie Why, the one who's coming to dinner, dear.
Marge (*off*) Why do I get dizzy, like I'm on a roundabout? You do know her name, I suppose?
Lottie Ivy.

Pause

Or Lily. Something botanical. Are you quite sure you wouldn't like to hear what I've written?
Marge (*off; sighing*) It's inevitable, isn't it?
Lottie (*reading*) "The rain pitter-pattered off Vanda's chic, Dior, plastic rainwear, shining like a scarlet beacon in the murky night."
Marge (*off*) I wish I'd been wearing chic Dior plastic.
Lottie (*reading*) "She gave a——"
Marge (*off*) Instead of that little number from Oxfam.
Lottie (*reading*) "She gave a delicate——"
Marge (*off*) Eighty-five per cent cotton, fifteen per cent polyester. Dior wouldn't use a mixture like that to clean his doorknob!
Lottie (*reading*) "She gave a——"
Marge (*off*) I might have been wearing a pocket handkerchief, for all the rain it kept off. I was soaked!
Lottie (*acidly*) I suppose we must be thankful you didn't lose your voice! (*She continues reading*) "She gave a delicate shudder, as the back of Louise du Cambray's head disintegrated."

Marge comes in from the kitchen

Marge The back of her head didn't exactly disintegrate——

Lottie Dramatic licence.

The pinger sounds

Marge (*on her way to the kitchen*) That'll be the leeks.

Marge goes into the kitchen

Lottie Damn the leeks! (*She continues reading*) "'How d'you feel, kiddo?' Tod asked her. Vanda's luminously pale, angelic features exuded a mere frisson of expression. 'Strangely exhilarated,' she told him, a slight tremor in her voice."
Marge (*off*) Did you feel strangely exhilarated?
Lottie I'm not Vanda Lane.
Marge (*off*) I deduced that when you mentioned luminously pale angelic features.

Pause

Lottie I felt nothing. Humping poor Violet's body around like a sack of potatoes sort of ... changed my viewpoint on death, I suppose. Come the end, we're just ... empty containers.
Marge (*off*) You feel no qualms about killing? I mean, in the case of Violet, someone else did the dirty work. But this time...
Lottie There was no malice: it was necessary.

Pause. Footsteps begin to descend the stairs, stop, then go up again

Do you have qualms?
Marge (*off*) I might: when I believe it's really happened.

The footsteps descend again and Ronnie enters. She wears a kerchief on her head, gipsy fashion, and has contrived a full-skirted outfit from bits of wardrobe belonging to the other ladies. She pirouettes, putting on large brass ear-rings

Marge peers round the kitchen door

Ronnie I almost forgot the ear-rings. Well? What do you think of me?
Marge That dress never looked like that on me.
Ronnie Well, I've taken the waist in by about a foot, and let out the bust——

Marge goes back into the kitchen

Lottie You look lovely, dear. Joe bought me those ear-rings in nineteen fifty-one—the year of the Festival of Britain. He liked me to look tarty, in those days. Later, he went mad over women in uniform. Were he alive today, it'd be traffic wardens. But then, were he alive today, I'd kill him!

Ronnie What happened?

Lottie He went fishing one morning and never came back.

Ronnie Drowned?

Lottie I like to think so.

Ronnie Then he might still be alive?

Lottie Don't be such a pessimist!

Marge enters, having removed her apron, and shaking a screw-top coffee jar covered in foil, containing ice and the ingredients for martinis

God! What elegance!

Marge (*pouring drinks*) A common-or-garden coffee jar, miraculously transformed, with the aid of kitchen foil, into a cocktail shaker. Tolpuddle Evening Institute, "Entertaining on a Budget", autumn, nineteen eighty-two. A good year for household management, eighty-two.

Marge goes into the kitchen to put the remainder back into the fridge

Lottie I thought it was to be *crème de menthe frappés*?

Marge (*off*) The green would have clashed with my frock.

Marge returns to the room and sits

Santé. I never did discover how Doris fiddled the books, you know.

Lottie A touch of genius in its sheer simplicity.

Ronnie She'd sneak stuff out of the store cupboard, prior to going out, then sell it back to us when she got home.

Lottie Hiding the loot in a money-belt, purchased for that precise purpose, from Oxfam.

Marge And did she confide where she hid her booze?

Ronnie Her window-box has a false bottom.

Marge (*affectionately*) Poor Doris: we'll miss her. (*Pointedly*) At least, some of us will. Frankly, Ronnie, there was something slightly obscene in the speed with which you got your clobber into her room, almost before we'd had the time to get out of our wet things.

Ronnie That front room's damned uncomfortable. I wasn't sleeping, and was becoming a nervous wreck!

Marge Nervous wreck? You're indestructible!

Lottie Girls! This is getting us nowhere.

Marge Very well, dear, let's get down to business. Who's coming to dinner?

Ronnie A woman named Rose.

Lottie I told you it was botanical.

Ronnie And she's quite old; in fact, even older than you two.

Marge Put together, or singly? I do hope you held a mirror to her lips, to make sure she was still breathing. Where did you find her?

Ronnie Tesco's.

Lottie Shoplifting. Ronnie caught her at it.

Ronnie I told her I'd seen her, made her put it in her basket, and then paid for it when we got to the check-out.

Marge *We* paid for it?

Ronnie It was only a small tin of salmon.

Lottie Red: she thinks pink rather *déclassé*. Besides, Sam won't touch anything but red.

Marge Then why doesn't Sam do his own shoplifting?

Ronnie He's next door's cat.

Marge She was shoplifting for a cat?

The others nod

I gather this ... unholy alliance extended beyond the check-out?

Ronnie I bought her a half pint of Guinness.

Marge From communal funds, of course!

Ronnie Business expenses: we've a situation here which must be exploited.

Lottie Ronnie has plans!

Ronnie She lives alone.

Lottie In a grotty old room, just like we used to. And she hasn't a soul in the world.

Marge Save for a cat, for which she's prepared to commit grand larceny.

Ronnie I felt sure, once you two had met her, you'd agree she was just right.

Marge For what? Holloway? Or the loony bin?

Ronnie For taking Doris's place, of course.

Lottie Just think, Marge: another pension book!

Marge We already have four: are you thinking of starting a collection?

Ronnie Now, ladies, just you listen to me. For some time now, wages have been rising faster than your pensions have——

Marge I wonder if they've found Doris yet?

Lottie Don't worry about her, Marge. She'll be having a whale of a time in that Great Tavern in the Sky!

Ronnie —which means that prices for just about everything which you don't nick——

Marge Which doesn't amount to a lot, then...

Ronnie —have been going up to the point where you soon won't be able to afford them.

Lottie Oxfam *never* put their prices up, and we wouldn't dream of nicking from them.

Ronnie But plenty of non-nickable, non-Oxfam essentials do go up … including your local taxes—and holidays!

Marge Holidays!

Lottie It means we're going to be a lot worse off, dear. No more holidays, probably.

Ronnie Lottie's right. And, since there's no-one fighting for the likes of you—the "have-nots"—it's up to us to use what imagination and cunning we can muster to maintain some decent standard of life. Let me outline what I have in mind. (*She consults some notes*) As I see it, our first five priorities are: one, a washing machine.

Lottie Oh, but I quite enjoy going to the launderette, I——

Ronnie Lottie, not having a washing machine is like not having an inside toilet. Something you do not mention in polite society. Besides, a woman of your age——

Lottie I chat to a woman there who's old enough to be my mother!

Ronnie Were that true, she'd be in a glass case in the British Museum. Priority number two: a proper freezer.

Marge The compartment at the top of the fridge——

Ronnie Is not a proper freezer. Bulk buying is far more economical. Also, we'll need the extra space to freeze part of the garden produce. Item three: a small greenhouse.

Lottie All sorts of really exotic plants can be grown in a small greenhouse. I read a very interesting article about some in a badly-printed magazine which fell out of the back pocket of a young man outside the Odeon as he was being chased by a policeman.

Marge Why was he being chased?

Lottie Haven't the faintest, dear. He seemed such a nice young man, who'd just been kind enough to help out a total stranger by giving him a twenty pound note for a bag of small change.

Marge Exotic greenhouse cultivation is bound to be available at the Tolpuddle. What are these plants you were reading about?

Lottie They must be one of those carnivorous plants—I think they're called cannibals.

Ronnie I don't think the Tolpuddle will be able to help much on that score, but you've certainly put an idea in my mind! Now, item four: a modest word processor.

Lottie Oh, that's hardly a priority.

Ronnie Kids of ten have them nowadays, so why shouldn't a woman of your … your… (*She flounders*)

Marge Decrepitude?

Ronnie Genius! You deserve something better than that clapped-out old typewriter upstairs. And I'm sure your ever-resourceful Evening Institute has a number of courses…

Lottie I'll check the prospectus tomorrow. Mind you, I'd probably need new glasses.

Marge Rose-tinted contact lenses would suit you wonderfully.

Lottie I must admit it would be nice to have something that worked.

Ronnie Now, item five: a microwave.

Lottie Don't be frivolous…

Ronnie You see, I'm anxious to get started on phase two, where we begin to get really ambitious.

Marge To me, a microwave is the very zenith of ambition. The crossing of the Rubicon. It will be with a rotisserie, won't it? And jet convection? And Auto Cook?

Ronnie I foresee, also, in the not-too-distant future, a sewing machine and a new second-hand car.

Lottie But Big Bella's like an old friend!

Ronnie An old friend with rust in her joints and a reluctance to climb hills.

Marge I have the same trouble myself.

Lottie But not the scrap heap? Not Big Bella?

Ronnie And… (*She pauses, holding them in suspense*)

Marge The *pièce de résistance* coming up?

Ronnie No more Bexhill-on-Sea. Next year, if all goes according to plan… I think…

Further pause

Lottie Stop tormenting us, you wicked thing!

Ronnie A spring holiday in…

Another pause

Marge Don't tell me! Let me guess! Somewhere truly exciting like … a holiday camp … where we can all enter for "knobbly knees" contests!

Lottie The Bahamas!

Marge We'd need to hijack an old people's outing to find enough pension books to finance that!

Ronnie Malta!

Pause

Lottie Why Malta?

Ronnie We've none of us been there … it's somewhere we may be able to afford … and very beautiful, I'm told…

Marge I wonder if the Tolpuddle does a course in Maltese?

Ronnie Then we're agreed it's time for a change?

Marge (*peering at the clock*) Excuse me, dear; d'you mind if we have the telly on? I'd like to hear the news summary, to see if there's anything about Doris. (*She gets up and switches it on*)

TV ...that high interest rates are a small price to pay...

Marge And it should be a microwave with an Easy Defrost.

TV ...unprecedented prosperity for all...

Lottie A change of scene might inspire a new novel.

The doorbell rings

Marge Dead on time!

Lottie Eight minutes early!

Marge Perhaps, when we reach phase three, we'll have matching gold watches.

TV ...the road-sweeper from Leicester, who had a record pools win of one million, eight hundred thousand pounds...

Ronnie Now, girls, we must all be on our very best behaviour and make her feel she'd like to come to live with us. And don't worry about the inconvenience. It won't be for long.

TV ..."It will make no difference to my life," he told our reporter...

The bell rings again

Marge My! but she's impatient!

TV ..."it's a vocation, the same as being a doctor".

Ronnie Bear in mind that it's through her that you're going to start to enjoy what others take for granted: that you're at last going to start to live like normal people.

Ronnie goes to open the front door, accompanied by Lottie

Marge goes into the kitchen, pushing the door to

TV ...woman found dead in Wittleborough Cemetery, with a bullet wound, has now been identified as Mrs Doris Cross, through a pension book she was carrying in a money-belt. The police say they are now pursuing a new line of enquiries. Well, that was a summary of the news, and it's now good-night from me, and over to the weather man. (*Another voice*) Well, there's no change, I'm afraid, and the deep depression over most of the country's going to continue: at least, for the present. Let me show you, on the chart, the areas worst hit...

The stage darkens

ACT II

Scene 1

Immediately following the end of Act I

The bell to the front door is heard to ring. The TV is still on

Lottie (*off*) God! She's impatient!
Ronnie (*off*) She's not due till eight!
Lottie (*off*) She's probably been starving herself for the occasion.

The door is heard to open and close, then a murmur of voices

> *Marge emerges from the kitchen with her "cocktail shaker". She switches off the TV*

> *Lottie and Ronnie enter from the hall with Grubb, a handsome man in his late thirties, with short fair hair*

(*To Marge*) This is Detective Inspector Grubb.
Grubb Good evening, ladies.
Marge Grubb? As in——?
Lottie As in food: as in nasty little wriggly things——
Grubb With two b's.
Marge You have my commiseration, Inspector. A policeman's lot is not a happy one, even under normal circumstances. But to be the victim of such a cruel practical joke! Tut, tut! Of course, had you been a police-woman——
Grubb I have never entertained any ambitions in that direction.
Marge —you would at least have had the option of changing such an unfortunate nomenclature: by marriage. (*She shakes the coffee jar at Grubb*) I don't suppose we can tempt you…?
Lottie When a dick's on the job——
Marge I think you should rephrase that remark, Lottie.
Grubb I try not to appear too stereotyped: so, what the hell. No-one's going to shop me, are they? (*He smiles, directing his charm at Ronnie*)

Marge pours him a drink

Marge Lottie talks in fifties clichés because——

Ronnie She writes detective novels.

Marge *A* detective novel. Which appears to have been in creation since World War One, or beyond!

Lottie *Baby, Here's Your Shroud!*

Grubb You must send me an autographed copy when it's published.

Marge You should live so long! Or, indeed, be so unfortunate as to be compromised into reading it!

Lottie The naked face of envy showing itself again!

Grubb (*indicating the table*) I hope I'm not interrupting anything?

Marge Just a very dear friend and neighbour dropping in for dinner. (*She hands him his drink*) There! Shaken, and not stirred!

Grubb (*sipping*) Ambrosia! Your health, ladies.

Ronnie (*to Marge*) The Inspector's here making enquiries about Doris.

Marge Drunk and disorderly again?

Slight pause

Grubb She's dead, I'm afraid.

Further pause

Lottie Dead?

Grubb This has no doubt come as a great shock.

Lottie We're all walking the tightrope between life and death, Inspector. Please excuse me, while I jot that down. (*She gets out her notebook and begins writing*)

Marge Lottie and I knew Doris. Ronnie's a more recent addition to the household.

Grubb (*gallantly*) A most attractive addition, if I might venture an opinion.

Ronnie You most certainly may. (*She gives a mock curtsy*) Thank you, kind sir.

Grubb (*smiling*) The pleasure's mine.

Lottie Ronnie's here visiting her grandmother.

Ronnie Except I missed her: she's away on a caravan holiday. At her age!

Grubb How old is she?

Marge Let's say she's ... in the departure lounge of life. But tell us more about poor Doris.

Grubb Her body was found, early this morning, in Yorkshire. Wittleborough Cemetery. She'd been shot.

Lottie Shot! How dramatic!

Marge A little over the top, even for Doris.

Ronnie From what you've told me, she was never a one for doing things by halves.

Marge An inborn flair for exaggeration: she was once a barmaid.
Lottie (*absently*) Barperson, I think, dear. (*To Grubb*) Could it have been a gangland killing?
Marge You think a pensioner of some seventy-years-plus double-crossed the Mafia in a million dollar heroin deal?
Lottie Could be she was scarpering with the loot. It's a well established practice, shooting welshers in the back of the head.
Grubb Who said anything about the back of the head?

Slight pause

Marge (*covering*) Sheer wishful thinking, on Lottie's part. That's how it would have happened in her … saga.
Grubb About Mrs Cross…
Lottie Funny: we never thought of her as Mrs Cross, did we, Marge?
Grubb Was this her address?
Marge Not any more.
Lottie Not for some time.
Grubb She was wearing a body-belt containing her pension book, with this address on it.

The three ladies laugh, and exchange glances

What's the joke?
Marge We had no idea she possessed a body-belt.
Lottie Come to think of it, there were times her waist looked decidedly lumpy: like an ill-distributed sack of Jaffa oranges.
Ronnie Well, if her pension book was still there, the motive obviously wasn't robbery.
Grubb We've yet to establish a motive. (*He takes out a notebook and a ballpoint pen*) When did she leave?
Marge (*shrugging and looking at the others*) Difficult to say. Three months ago?
Lottie Went out one morning, and never came back. A quick "cheery pip" and she was gone.
Grubb Did you report her missing?
Lottie No, but we weren't expecting her back.
Grubb Why not?

Pause

Lottie (*inventing*) Her geraniums!
Grubb (*nonplussed*) Her geraniums…?

Lottie They were all over the floor: we felt she'd burned her bridges.

Ronnie I'm told she grew them in a window-box with a false bottom.

Lottie Specially designed to conceal her booze.

Marge Contraband booze.

Lottie You see, Inspector, she bought it with money she filched from the household accounts. It had to be hidden somewhere. There were days she could hardly stagger down the stairs.

Marge Obviously, once she'd revealed the hiding place, she'd reached ... the point of no return.

Slight pause

Ronnie (*inventing*) The last that was heard of her, she was living at Waterloo. Cardboard City.

Lottie (*gilding the lily*) In a cardboard box.

Ronnie (*enjoying herself*) Living in sin!

Grubb In a cardboard box?

Lottie A large cardboard box.

Marge She prided herself on being one of the last of the true Bohemians. Would spend hours, down at the library, reading *The New Statesman*.

Grubb Can you think of anyone who might have borne her a grudge?

Lottie A jealous lover, perhaps?

Ronnie Really, Lottie! She was over seventy!

Lottie Who knows what fiery passions throbbed in that shrivelled bosom?

Marge Well, I don't think I'd venture as far as "fiery passions", Lottie. Faint stirrings, perhaps, whilst under the influence.

Lottie She didn't get on at all well with that fat woman in the sub post office.

Marge Mrs Withers?

Lottie Miss Withers.

Ronnie The one with pebble glasses an inch thick?

Marge Precisely! I doubt she could hit an elephant from a distance of six feet!

Grubb Were there any relatives?

Lottie Not that we know of.

Grubb Can you give me a more ... accurate date as to when she left here?

Lottie (*suddenly and firmly*) June the twenty-first!

Marge and Ronnie are taken aback by her vehemence

Grubb How can you be so sure?

Lottie Summer solstice, the longest day of the year. It happened to fall on the day I collect my pension.

Grubb And that was the last any of you saw of her?

Lottie Yes.

Grubb Then how did you know she was living in a cardboard box?

Very slight pause

Lottie (*inspired*) Ah! Connie Lampitt!
Grubb Connie Lampitt?
Ronnie Our Chief Librarian.
Lottie She saw her, and couldn't resist rushing back to tell everyone how poor Doris was now a homeless, hopeless wino!
Grubb Did she speak to Mrs Cross?
Marge Oh, she's not *that* avant-garde. Under her cultivated "thirties Bloomsbury" look lurks a blue rinse fighting to get out.

The doorbell rings

Lottie That'll be Pansy.
Ronnie Rose.

Ronnie goes into the hall and returns with Rose, a woman in her seventies, dressed entirely in black, save for a large bunch of very red, very shiny, very plastic cherries on her hat

Rose Sorry I'm late, but I had to nip into a supermarket to pick up Sam's breakfast.
Ronnie (*to Grubb*) Sam's her next door neighbour's cat. Rose—this is Lottie—she's the novelist—and this is Marge.
Rose What do you do?
Marge Offhand? Spanish dancing, macramé, Italian, French, picture framing, karate, dried-flower arranging——
Ronnie Thanks to Marge's insatiable quest for knowledge, they've been able to keep on the entire staff at the Tolpuddle Evening Institute!
Marge —creative cookery, furniture restoration, archery, origami——
Ronnie She's even mastered the contrabassoon.
Lottie (*sweetly*) Isn't it a pity we can't afford one?
Rose And who's he?
Ronnie Detective Inspector Grubb.
Rose (*very agitated*) What's he doing here? Who asked him? I've been shopped! It's a trap! Which one of you is an agent provocative? A trap! You told me dinner, but said——
Ronnie He's come to tell us that a friend of Marge and Lottie has died.
Rose They don't look very bereaved. When's the burial taking place?
Marge Is that important?
Rose Well, I mean, I'll go to the funeral, if you're too busy: seeing as she was

a friend of yours. Of course, I'd need to check my diary: I've three during the coming week. No. I tell a lie: four. People seem to be dropping like flies at the moment. Something to do with the fall of the leaves, I expect. Of course, I prefer proper burials, with people being popped into holes in the ground, but I have been known to take on a crematorium event, even though I always feel the atmosphere's a bit like death warmed up. As a matter of fact, I've been to a funeral this very afternoon.

Lottie Oh dear. Someone close?

Rose Didn't know the woman from Adam. Just happened to be passing, felt a little peckish, so nipped in. Well, it's company, isn't it? And it saves burning electricity in the flat. Smoked salmon, today. End pieces, I regret to say: not slices. I might have guessed it was being done on the cheap. Only a couple of wreaths: the rest, sprays of chrysanths, with the odd tiger lily thrown in to create the illusion of opulence. But it gave me a chance to show off the new hat.

Lottie Don't people mind you ... just butting in?

Rose Each side of the family thinks I'm a poor relation, belonging to the other, so wouldn't dream of questioning my presence; no more than they'd speak ill of the dead. Of course, the cherries weren't on the hat when I bought it. From Oxfam. No, I tell a lie; Imperial Cancer Research. I got the cherries in Woolworths.

Marge (*making conversation*) Oh, you bought those in Woolworths, did you?

Rose (sotto voce) No: I said I got them in Woolworths. I wonder if I could go and powder my nose and take my coat off? It's warm in here.

Lottie Of course. I'll show you the way.

Rose Nice to have met you, Inspector Glib.

Grubb Grubb.

Ronnie With two bs.

Lottie leads Rose off and upstairs

Marge I suppose I ought really to see what's happening to the food. Unless my presence is urgently required?

Grubb (*looking at his watch*) We'll have to continue this tomorrow, in any case. I've another appointment at half past eight.

Marge goes into the kitchen, pushing the door to

Pause

There's something not quite ... kosher ... about those old ladies.

Ronnie A bit eccentric, I grant you...

Grubb Eccentric? Stone bonkers!

Slight pause

Or are they really as crazy as they'd like me to think?

Pause

How did they know she'd been shot in the head? The *back* of the head?
Ronnie Pure guesswork.
Grubb And this ... Rose. How come Lottie can't even remember her name,
if she's such an old friend and neighbour?
Ronnie Absent-mindedness! At their age——
Grubb And if she's a friend and neighbour of *theirs*, here at *their* invitation,
how come *you* made all the introductions?
Ronnie It just appeared that way——
Grubb As if they'd never seen her before in their lives!
Ronnie (*false laugh*) Really, Inspector——
Grubb And why do you avoid answering my questions?
Ronnie Are you seriously suggesting you think those two harmless old
ladies had something to do with Doris's death?
Grubb They could be homicidal maniacs, under all their barminess, for all
I know! Up to their lavender-scented armpits in decomposing bodies!
Ronnie Then I'd like to know where they're hiding 'em. Not out in the yard,
certainly, because I've been digging it over to start a vegetable garden.
Grubb Are you sure you weren't the one who invited Rose to dinner?
Ronnie Why would I lie about a thing like that?
Grubb You tell me.
Ronnie Why didn't you ask *her*, while she was here?
Grubb Maybe I will, when she comes down.

Pause

And another thing——
Ronnie You've nice eyes: d'you know that?
Grubb Yes. The business of——
Ronnie Sort of sexy.
Grubb Yes. That business——
Ronnie And you've the sort of hair I could run through barefoot!

Marge enters from the kitchen

Marge A quick dash to the little girls' room is called for while the peas are
on the boil.

Marge rushes into the hall and up the stairs

Ronnie Don't you ever have any mad urges?
Grubb There's a time and place——
Ronnie Fiery uncontrollable lusts?
Grubb Look, miss——
Ronnie Call me Ronnie.
Grubb All that crap about the cardboard box——
Ronnie Is there no romance in your soul? Why "crap"?
Grubb What woman of seventy is going to give up a warm, comfortable place like this to go to live like a tramp?
Ronnie (*shrugging*) Maybe, like you, she didn't want to be stereotyped. Anyway, sexpot, why didn't you question it *then*, when it was mentioned?
Grubb I was anxious to know to what depths of fantasy they were prepared to go. To what depths you were *all* prepared to go!
Ronnie I bet you're not married. You're one of the untamed: like my father. He didn't marry, either. Well, that's not strictly true. He married nearly every woman he ever shook hands with.
Grubb (*impatiently*) This is all very interesting——
Ronnie Yes: I thought you'd find it so. Whereas other men had a post-coital cigarette, he seemed to prefer a marriage ceremony. I was conceived against a pub wall. *The Knave of Hearts*. A bit like my father, really. An absolute charmer, from all accounts. But then, so are you.
Grubb Another thing——
Ronnie Can you keep a secret?
Grubb —what did Rose mean when she said she'd been trapped?
Ronnie I've an irresistible urge to nibble your ear!
Grubb (*sharply*) What's all this Delilah routine?
Ronnie Delilah? In this outfit? I feel more like a renegade from a gypsy orchestra!
Grubb You wouldn't, by any chance, be attempting to pervert the course of justice?
Ronnie Don't tell me! You're incorruptible!
Grubb No-one's incorruptible: it's a question of price.

Pause

If those old ladies did it——
Ronnie I refuse to be part of such a ludicrous discussion!
Grubb —*why* did they do it? And, if they did, what happened to the other one? Your grandmother.
Ronnie I've told you——

Footsteps on the stairs. Marge enters

Marge I do hope you're not grilling Ronnie too savagely, Inspector. Our vines have tender grapes. Rose has decided to have a little pre-dinner nap, so won't see you before you go, but sent her regards.

Marge goes into the kitchen, pushing the door to

Grubb (*looking at his watch*) It looks as if I'll have to continue this interview some other time. (*He rises from his seat*) What about tomorrow morning?
Ronnie Can't wait!
Grubb Eleven o'clock?
Ronnie (*standing very close to him*) I shall count each minute until then, Inspector.
Grubb Gus.
Ronnie Gus?
Grubb Augustus.
Ronnie Augustus Grubb?
Grubb It gets worse: Augustus Gregory.
Ronnie Augustus Gregory Grubb? (*She smiles*) Your parents must have hated you! (*She lightly kisses his forehead and moves away*)
Grubb What's Ronnie short for?
Ronnie Veronica.
Grubb I prefer Veronica: Ronnie sounds … sort of criminal.
Ronnie (*softly, with a smile*) You've just suggested that I *am* a criminal. An accessory, at least. (*She taps on the kitchen door*) The Inspector's just about to leave.

Marge comes in from the kitchen

Marge (*emerging*) Everything's curling at the edges, and looking quite disgusting. It'll certainly be a meal to remember. I do hope you've had … an instructive time with Ronnie?
Grubb I'll come back tomorrow morning, when I hope to find you not so busy.
Ronnie At eleven o'clock.
Marge Elevenses! I must bring out the garibaldis!

Ronnie goes into the hall with Grubb

Grubb (*off*) Until tomorrow, then.
Ronnie (*off*) I wait with baited breath!

The front door opens and closes

Ronnie enters

Marge The big seduction scene was hardly *Romeo and Juliet*, was it?

Ronnie Had I known you were listening, I'd have done it in blank verse.

Marge Just as well I *was* listening. How else could we have warned Lottie to keep Rose out of the way until he'd gone?

Ronnie You think she'd have squealed?

Marge Like one of Lottie's "chicks"!

Ronnie Not that she knows that much.

Marge He's suspicious already. It wouldn't have taken long for him to discover she's not an old friend at all, but a crazy shoplifter you acquired in Tesco's.

Pause

Ronnie What are we going to do with her?

Marge Feed her, send her home, and have a council of war.

Marge goes to the bottom of the stairs

(*Off; calling*) All clear, girls, and dinner's almost ready.

Marge returns to the living-room

Almost ready for the dustbin! Of course, much depends upon how corrupt he is, and how far you're prepared to go to get him off our backs.

Ronnie (*smiling*) Am I to be offered as a human sacrifice?

Marge After such short acquaintance I've not decided yet whether you're human or not. As for the sacrifice, since you were prepared to run barefoot through his hair, I'd have assumed sleeping with him to be a mere formality.

Footsteps on the stairs. Rose and Lottie enter

Rose Which would be my room, if I came to live here?

Marge (*pouring her a drink*) Well, it wasn't actually … a definite offer.

Rose (*surprised*) Oh, but it was. Ronnie said——

Ronnie Not *definite*!

Rose (*calmly*) Don't argue, dear. Most definite. You said the place is run as a co-operative, and that if I put my pension book into the kitty, and did the odd chore, I'd be housed, fed, and have no bills to worry about. All I can attribute your sloppy thinking to, child, are those two half pints of stout you slurped your way through. I felt, at the time, you were overly ambitious, and should have ordered lemonade shandy.

Marge hands her her drink

Thank you, dear. (*She sips it*) Ah! Dry martini! How very civilized! Cheers! (*She drains her glass and puts it down*) Where was I? Oh, yes. I gave the matter some thought, and, like in all things, coming here has both its advantages and its disadvantages. On the credit side, I'd be just a stone's throw away from the crematorium, and at least three large hospitals; but, on the debit side, what'll happen to Sam?

Ronnie The people next door would have to look after him, themselves.

Marge *If* we made a definite offer.

Rose (*slowly*) I suppose I could ... occasionally take round some food for him...

Marge No! We have our reputations to think of, Rose; and if you were living here in the house, and got caught shoplifting crates of cat food——

Lottie Not cat food, dear, pink salmon.

Rose Red: he won't touch pink. And who can blame him? Pink's only fit for making fish cakes!

Marge The shade is——

Rose And no way do I intend standing over a hot stove making fish cakes for a cat!

Marge I was thinking more of the risk you take——

Rose Oh, there's no risk. I've done it for years, and was taught by one of the best in the business. A little social worker from Bermondsey. Lovely woman: it was rumoured she could carry her own body-weight in loot without a hint of detection.

Pause

(*Smiling nostalgically*) Ah, you don't see those lovely interlock knickers advertised like you used to, with double gussets, and thick elastic round the bottoms of the legs. You could get a week's groceries in 'em, if you'd the legs to carry it home.

Pause

Well? Are we going to eat? (*She glances sharply at Marge and Ronnie*) Or was that not a definite offer, either?

Marge (*on her way to the kitchen*) You certainly have a winning way with you, don't you?

Marge goes into the kitchen

Rose Which is my seat?

Lottie Oh ... any one.

Rose sits at the table

Rose Of course, I shouldn't have been at that funeral this afternoon: it was pure self-indulgence. I should have been sitting with my neighbour, Carlotta, who has this very nasty ear infection. It's too dreadful for words! (*She looks at the stitching on the back of her napkin*) These aren't very well finished off, are they? You shouldn't have all these untidy bits of cotton dangling about.

Marge enters with a tureen of soup, and bread

I suppose they're something Marge did down at that institute of hers...
Marge (*with a big smile*) So, who'd like a nice tomato rinse, then?

The stage darkens

<h1 style="text-align:center">SCENE 2</h1>

Ten forty-five the following morning

The clock strikes the three-quarters. Lottie sits at the table, her novel before her. Her cheek rests on her hand, and she almost dozes. Marge sits with her Fair Isle knitting on her lap, tiredly staring ahead. She yawns

Ronnie, wearing jeans and an old sweater, enters from the kitchen bearing a tray with three cups of coffee, which she distributes

Lottie I thought she'd never go home!
Ronnie She's certainly got a lot of life in her!
Marge Alas, yes; and it'll have to stay in her now that Grubb's seen her.
Lottie So much for all our lovely plans.

They sip their coffee

Ronnie D'you think we actually managed to discourage her from coming to live here?
Marge Who knows? I certainly tried, by telling her that, due to cuts in the Health Service, two of the local hospitals are likely to get the chop.
Lottie She wasn't listening: she was far too busy going on about the discharge from Carlotta's ear.
Ronnie All through the charlotte russe!
Marge No, child: during the charlotte russe we had the revolting symptoms shown by her neighbours' fantails when they were mysteriously struck down by pigeon pox! (*She sips her coffee*)

Lottie I think our proximity to the crematorium appears the main attraction for her.

Marge What possible reason could I give for that ceasing to exist?

Ronnie We could always say it burned down!

Pause

Maybe she'll decide we're all very boring people?

Marge Speak for yourself: Lottie and I aren't boring. (*She sips her coffee*) A little ... subdued at times, perhaps...

Pause

If one looks on the bright side, at least she made no mention of coming again, did she?

Ronnie It was the drink: she was paralytic! Didn't even say good-night.

Lottie (*yawning*) There was a prowler in the garden during the night.

Marge You're always hearing prowlers.

Ronnie What's there to steal, anyway?

Lottie Big Bella?

Ronnie (*laughing*) That old banger wouldn't interest even the most desperate car thief!

Lottie (*vaguely*) Someone might have been looking for a ... getaway car!

Marge Has it gone?

Lottie No.

Marge Which proves he couldn't even get it away from the kerb. Pity. The insurance might have got us something a little younger.

Lottie You mean, like a nineteen sixty model?

Marge (*considering her knitting*) D'you know, I seem to have forgotten what it is I'm making: and it seemed such a good idea at the time. I know it has pyramids and camels and armholes...

Lottie Talking of starting things, I've started on a new novel.

Marge You've actually finished *Baby, Here's Your Shroud*?

Lottie I've decided to put it into cold storage, and try something more contemporary. Something based on real life! Would you like to hear a bit of it?

Marge (*to Ronnie*) That's what's known as a rhetorical question. The Day of Reckoning couldn't stop her!

Lottie (*reading*) "Police Sergeant Gus Gimbo——"

Ronnie Gus? Inspired by Gus Grubb?

Lottie (*determinedly*) "Police Sergeant Gus Gimbo, of the NYPD"—that's the New York Police Department——

Marge (*winking*) Gotcha!

Lottie (*reading*) "—was a dick no decent-minded dame would care to handle. A dick destined to stand up and be counted, come hell or high water. Until that fateful day he brushed with luscious Mimsie Mickleheimer, a classy broad who happened to be the daughter of the sinister mafioso boss, Pinky the Punk. 'You sure do send me, babe,' Gus told her, his voice a dark brown growl, his coal black eyes a hungry consuming flame as she jumped down, revealing a tantalising glimpse of cool alabaster thighs."

Marge Jumped down where?

Lottie From his desk.

Marge I find it ambiguous. She could be jumping down from anything. A hot air balloon, for instance.

Lottie In Police Precinct Zero Zero Seven? You're not concentrating.

Marge That's true. This is the row where I start to decrease for the neck, or armhole, or whatever. Purely from a technical point of view, in what way, precisely, does this sexy sergeant differ from Tod Mallet, your previous hero?

Lottie Gus is crooked.

Marge Ah! Gotcha!

Lottie Crooked as a corkscrew. As Gus's ravishing sidekick, Sergeant Phyllida Pepperoni said of him, on a previous page: "'I've a hunch that fink is crooked, and there's nothing pisses me off more than a bent dick!'"

Ronnie Why did you say it was a fateful day when he met Mimsie Oojamaflip?

Lottie Because she's acting as a decoy to take Gus's attention from her father, who's iced a couple of guys.

Marge I see what you mean about basing it on real life. (*To Ronnie*) I hope you're the proud possessor of alabaster thighs: they seem a main essential to the plot.

Ronnie But you've not "iced a couple of guys." Violet's death was natural.

Marge Well, as natural as death *can* be, after a few blows to the head with a blunt instrument.

Ronnie I mean, you didn't actually kill her.

Lottie Agreed, but we've gone on drawing her pension.

Marge Which probably carries a far heavier penalty than wholesale manslaughter!

Lottie Nor did we report her demise.

Marge That would have been a fate worse than death! They'd have come and taken back her pension book!

Pause

Ronnie Pity about Doris's pension book.

Marge That was utter carelessness: we should have checked her body-belt before dashing back into the car.

Lottie You mustn't blame yourself, Marge: it was pouring down with rain.
Marge I had no intention of blaming myself!
Lottie Well, you can stop looking at me!
Marge My pleasure!
Ronnie That leaves only me, doesn't it?
Marge No-one's to blame, Ronnie. Oh, that is to say, we all are. We all knew she had a body-belt.
Lottie But who would have expected her to steal her book out of the community chest like that?

Pause

Her heart was never really in it, you know: being part of a co-operative.
Marge And our brave new world so depended upon continuing to draw her pension!

Pause

Ronnie Poor Doris: she died for nothing, in the end, didn't she? Her departure hasn't furthered our cause one little bit, has it?
Marge (*wistfully*) Goodbye microwave, with your jet convection and rotisserie!
Lottie (*wistfully*) Goodbye modest word processor.

Pause

Goodbye to our chances of progressing into the world of the living. Now that Grubb's seen her, no way can Rose suddenly disappear from the face of the earth!
Ronnie Cheer up, girls: we'll just have to do a little re-planning, that's all.
Marge If there's one thing I can do without, it's Ronnie sounding like a cheerful hockey mistress!
Ronnie Look on the bright side. At least you've got me to do a Myrtle Micklethingy——
Lottie Mimsie Mickleheimer.
Ronnie ——on Inspector Grubb, who seems very interested.
Lottie But is it ethical?
Marge Is what ethical?
Lottie Ronnie having to offer up her virtue on our account.
Marge If you're really talking about virtue, Lottie, there's a great deal of virtue in Ronnie giving vent to sheer unbridled passion for the sake of the co-operative. If, on the other hand, you're referring to chastity, not many young people of today would agree with you regarding its value as a virtue.
Lottie It's different for Mimsie to give her all: she's a tramp.

Ronnie Maybe I am, at heart. Could be something I've inherited from my
father. I've never given vent to unbridled passion: maybe I'll enjoy it!
Lottie You don't have to go that far. Just close your eyes——
Marge And think of electrical appliances!

The doorbell rings

Ronnie That's him, I expect. Now, don't forget, girls: he doesn't believe a
word you've told him.

Ronnie goes into the hall, opens the door and admits Grubb

(*Off*) Good morning, sexy.

Grubb enters the room, followed by Ronnie

Lottie Good morning, Sergeant Gimbo.
Grubb Detective Inspector Grubb. Good morning, ladies.
Marge Gimbo's the one with the dark brown voice, in Lottie's new book.
Lottie *Requiem For A Squealing Chick!*
Ronnie (*to Grubb*) I'll get you some coffee.

Ronnie goes into the kitchen

Marge (*calling after her*) Don't forget the garibaldis, dear. (*To Grubb*) Do
sit down.

He sits

Lottie If you're still investigating Doris's death, has the possibility of suicide
not occurred to you, Inspector?
Marge She was shot in the back of the head.

Pause

Lottie She had very long arms. For a woman of her height.
Grubb Why are you so insistent upon that?
Lottie The length of her arms?
Grubb Her being shot in the back of the head.
Marge Was she? So you were right after all, Lottie. Have you discovered any
clues, Inspector?
Grubb I'd prefer to discuss the matter when we're all here.
Lottie To be perfectly honest——
Grubb Which, pardon me, ladies, you have not been——

Lottie I am still of the opinion the crime is drug-related.

Ronnie enters and gives coffee to Grubb. She places the biscuits on the table

Ronnie (*seating herself*) Any new developments?

Slight pause

Grubb With regard to your grandmother...
Ronnie What's she got to do with it?
Grubb Have you heard from her since you've been here?
Ronnie No, but Marge and Lottie have. She doesn't know I'm here.
Lottie We get postcards all the time.
Grubb Then I wonder if you'd be so good as to show me one or two?
Lottie Oh, we don't keep them: they're so boring!
Marge Violet has a God-given gift for finding the dullest card the resort has to offer within seconds of arrival!

Slight pause

Grubb In other words, you have absolutely no proof of where she is?

Slight pause

   Or even if she's still alive?
Lottie Why shouldn't she be alive?
Ronnie Yes, what are you getting at?

Slight pause

Grubb This ... alleged caravan holiday...
Lottie Alleged?
Grubb Did she go alone?
Marge She's accompanied by a male admirer.
Grubb (*getting out his notebook*) Perhaps you could give me his name?

Slight pause

Marge (*positively*) Dinkums!

Grubb looks at her

   That's all she ever called him.

Lottie (*getting in on the act*) Sometimes it was darling Dinkums. Or ickle Dinkums. Or——

Grubb May I hazard a guess that you're unable to give me an address for this ... Mr Dinkums?

Marge Sorry. Somewhere with a ring of romance to it, I seem to remember.

Lottie Try Penge.

Pause. She gives Grubb a frail smile

You'd expect us to be ... more co-operative, being a co-operative, wouldn't you?

Pause. Grubb grins

Grubb Tut tut, ladies: you'll never make master criminals. (*He takes a plastic bag from his pocket; containing a revolver*) And which of you ladies, might I ask, was careless enough to leave this little trinket in the glove compartment of the car?

Lottie It's a frame-up! (*To Marge*) I told you I heard a prowler. Little did I realize it was the fuzz! (*To Grubb*) You're lucky I didn't call the police and have you arrested! I hope you had a warrant to search that car?

Grubb (*unperturbed*) Does it belong to any of you?

Lottie It's community property, if that's what you mean.

Marge At least, it was, until it was stolen.

Lottie By the man who came to read the meter, we think.

Marge Is it the murder weapon?

Grubb It hasn't been to ballistics yet.

Lottie The whole thing's crystal clear. The man from the electricity board killed Doris—a *crime passionnel*, I suspect—and is now trying to frame us for the murder. All we have to do is——

Ronnie (*firmly*) Let me speak to the Inspector, alone. (*To Grubb*) If that's OK with you, Gus?

Lottie That's a highly irregular suggestion!

Grubb This is a highly irregular situation.

Ronnie It's all right, Lottie: I'm a big girl now.

Lottie (*rising*) Then shall we——

Ronnie We can talk in the front room: it'll save disturbing you. (*To Grubb*) You don't mind?

Grubb Suits me fine. (*To the others*) Don't——

Lottie We know. Don't leave town, we may be subpoenaed!

Grubb (*smiling*) I was going to say, don't worry about Ronnie; she'll be all right.

Ronnie (*smiling*) How disappointing. I thought I might indulge in a little improper activity whilst helping the police with their enquiries!

Grubb laughs

Grubb and Ronnie exit

Pause

Lottie What if I were to go to ... say Bexhill ... and send a postcard with a message from Violet on it? He doesn't know her handwriting.
Marge It's a little too late for that, I'm afraid. He knows.

Pause

But I wonder what he intends doing about it?

The doorbell rings

Lottie goes and opens the door to admit Rose, carrying a small case and a birdcage with a cloth over it

Rose puts the cage on a side table

Rose I just thought I'd bring Polly over, with a few essentials, to start with.
Lottie (*following her in*) But we hadn't establ——
Rose Of course, you'll have to learn to keep your hands away from the cage: he's got a nasty nip with him. Loves fingers! Can't get enough of 'em. Noses, too, if you're fool enough to stick it between the bars.
Marge I'm glad you warned me: sticking my nose through the bars of birdcages is a little weakness of mine!
Lottie But, Rose: nothing was agreed——
Rose It's the room at the front, isn't it?
Lottie Ronnie's in there, at the moment, with——
Rose In that case, I'll just tidy up a bit, then come down and have a cup of coffee and a biscuit. (*She picks up a biscuit, feels it, and drops it back on the plate*) Just coffee will do. (*To Marge*) Did you embroider that tablecloth?
Marge (*defensively*) Yes.
Rose Mmmm! Thought so. Look after Polly. And for heaven's sake don't give him any of those biscuits!

Rose goes into the hall and up the stairs

Lottie and Marge look at each other in bewilderment, then burst into laughter. The stage darkens

SCENE 3

Half an hour later

*Marge and Lottie are in the living-room, drinking tea and looking despond-
ent. Lottie stares at her unopened notebook whilst Marge stares at her
knitting. On the table stands a tray containing a teapot, extra cup, milk, etc.*

Lottie Rose has been up there a long time: what do you suppose she's doing?
Marge Stealing the bathroom fittings, I shouldn't wonder.

*Pause. Suddenly inspired, Lottie opens her book and begins feverishly
writing*

> *Rose descends the stairs during Lottie's speech and enters the room,
> clutching her pension book*

Lottie (*reading as she writes*) "Sergeant Phyllida Pepperoni smoothed her
uniform across her inviting thighs and threw her dazzling smile across the
room. Gus's eyes caught hers, and, as if at a given signal, they bounced
toward the squad car. His dark brown voice was a mere seductive growl.
'Let's grab a fistful of chow, babe,' he whispered."

Rose peers beneath the cloth into the parrot's cage

Rose I hope you've not been feeding Polly: he's looking a bit green about
the gills!
Marge I didn't dare. I need all my fingers to decrease for the armhole.
Rose (*handing her pension book to Lottie*) The water was so nice and hot I
decided to have a bath while I was up there.
Lottie (*looking at the pension book*) It says "Mrs".
Rose Ah, that's because I was married. (*She pours herself some tea*) Sidney
passed on eight years ago.
Lottie You poor thing!
Rose Oh, he was very well insured: I saw to that. Of course, the payments
were a bit steep, but ... well, you have to look upon it as ... an investment,
don't you? A bit like doing the pools, really. You pays your money each
week, then sits back to wait for the jackpot.
Marge What if you'd died first?
Rose I had no intention of doing any such thing! (*She sips her tea*) He went
over a cliff. (*She sits*) It was quite amusing, really. Once I'd got over the
shock, that is. I was busy attending to a small blister on my heel, at the time.
One minute, there he was, large as life, belching after a breakfast

containing enough cholesterol to kill a battalion, and the next, he was gone!
  (*She snaps her fingers*) Just like that!
Lottie How awful!
Rose Bereavement doesn't come easy. Especially when you've a perfectly
  good return ticket going to waste. But, like they say, every cloud has a silver
  lining. I was fortunate enough to find a sticking plaster in my bag, so at least
  I didn't have a septic heel on top of everything else. (*She sips her tea*) He'd
  always expressed the desire that when he went he hoped it would be quick.
  Well, he'd have been hard pushed to have found a quicker end than that!
  Whoosh! Plummeted like a stone.

Pause

Marge For how long had you been married?
Rose Forty-three years.
Lottie You must have missed him.
Rose I must admit it would have been nice to have had him with me on the
  two world cruises I did; but then, had he still been alive, I would never have
  had the money to go in the first place. You can't have everything, can you?
  (*She sips her tea*) Where's Ronnie? Still occupying my room?
Lottie She's gone for a drink with the Inspector at *The Knave of Hearts*. Then
  she's bringing him back for a spot of lunch.
Rose A couple of halves of stout and she'll come back in no fit state to eat!
  Why are you feeding him?
Marge We're helping him with his enquiries.
Rose Is he still on about that Doreen?
Marge Doris.
Rose There's something fishy about her death, if you ask me, and if it's foul
  play it's usually the nearest and dearest who do it. Did you know that? (*She
  stands up*) Oh, well, I can't sit here gossiping all day: it's time for Polly's
  singing lesson.
Lottie (*incredulously*) Singing lesson?
Rose He has quite a nice voice, really. Just needs a bit of training.
Marge Dare one ask what you're teaching him to sing?
Rose "Nessun dorma", to start off with. Once he's mastered that I'll try him
  on some Schubert *lieder*. (*She picks up the cage and heads for the kitchen*)
  Later, when I've given him his breakfast, I'll go out on a little shopping
  spree, I think. So, if there's anything you need, just jot it down.

Rose takes the cage into the garden

Lottie That's all we need to turn the place into a madhouse. An operatic
  parrot!

Marge I hope that didn't blind you to her passing reference to a shopping spree. And what do you suppose she'll bring back, stuffed down those double-gussetted, interlock knickers?

Lottie A little Lapsang Souchong tea would be rather nice.

Marge Lottie! Don't encourage her! We've problems enough on our plate, without adding shoplifting to our list of crimes!

Lottie Short of bodily tossing her out on her ear—complete with the avian Pavarotti—we're stuck with her, so might as well make the most of it!

Marge I do not intend that we make the most of her light-fingered proclivity. Nor any other of her criminal achievements!

Lottie (*dreamily*) She could also stuff down the said knickers a few of the little delicacies we can't afford. Like fillet steak, and fresh rainbow trout, and artichokes, and ogee melons, and——

Marge (*emphatically*) No!

Pause

Lottie Do you suppose Sidney really fell?

Marge Not for a moment.

Lottie You think he was … helped over the cliff?

Marge With malice aforethought.

Pause

Lottie She certainly appears to have had much to gain.

Marge The insurance must have been enormous to finance her round the world twice.

Pause

Oh, what are we going to do about her?

Lottie ponders on this

Lottie When the rich get caught shoplifting, they get away with it because their lawyers put in pleas of kleptomania and the like, suggesting their clients are round the twist. Couldn't we try something like that? Cop a plea of diminished responsibility?

Marge I ask one thing only, dear: not to be in the same room when you put that suggestion to Rose. Not even in the same street, if possible.

A key is heard in the lock, and a moment later Ronnie, somewhat merry, and Grubb enter

Lottie Did Ronnie show you the wall?

Grubb (*smirking*) Yes.

Ronnie (*giggling*) He suggested we try it for ourselves, sometime.

Grubb Won't be easy, mind you: they've stuck a bicycle rack in the way.

Lottie The course of true love never did run smooth.

Marge If we're swapping clichés, Lottie, love will find a way. I once knew a teacher of English Lit who could perform, with consummate artistry, in her baby's perambulator, given three quarters of a bottle of gin and a randy sailor. It ruined the springs, needless to say.

Grubb (*sitting*) Now, let's stop beating about the bush, ladies. By the way, where's Rose?

Marge In the garden, giving her parrot a singing lesson.

Grubb Then leave her there for the moment.

Ronnie Gus has promised to help us.

Lottie What have you told him?

Grubb I didn't need to be told much. It seemed obvious the unknown body they'd previously found in that same cemetery was Violet's.

Lottie Not necessarily, dear: there could be a serial killer on the loose. There's a lot of 'em about at the moment.

Ronnie Look, Lottie: Gus knows what's been going on.

Grubb (*smiling*) But don't worry. I can fix it so that the powers-that-be won't link up the two bodies.

Marge How?

Grubb Favours: that's the name of the game. I've a couple of buddies in most areas, who owe me. I scratch their backs, they scratch mine. If we can't protect our friends in time of need, what's the point in having a bit of authority? It's one of the perks of the job.

Marge But how can you help us?

Grubb (*shrugging*) Records can go missing … the murder weapon, in the case of Doris, simply fails to turn up. As for the pension book and body-belt … they get hopelessly misfiled.

Pause

(*Smiling*) Why should I make problems for you? You didn't even kill her, anyway. Violet, that is. And as for Doris, well, ladies, you certainly had a bit of a teaser there, and, if I might say so, think you acted with great initiative!

Lottie (*suspiciously*) What's in it for you to keep your trap shut?

Grubb (*taking hold of Ronnie's hand*) Let's call it … a friendly gesture. After all, I'm almost one of the family, aren't I? (*He lightly kisses Ronnie*) If you're thinking I'm out to blackmail you—just look at it this way. What could you possibly offer me that could in any way compare with the "tributes" collected by yours truly from some of our more affluent transgressors, simply for looking the other way when they performed their little "contraventions of the law"? No, ladies, you've nothing to fear. Gus can afford a little charity.

Ronnie You see? All we could offer him would be mere chicken feed!

Marge Go upstairs and wash out your mouth, child: you're beginning to sound like Lottie!

Grubb If, however, you feel you'd like to show a bit of gratitude at any time, well, it'd be nice to share a good home-cooked meal with you every now and then.

Ronnie Gus has no family of his own: so you see, he could do with a little bit of mothering.

Lottie No family at all?

Grubb Both my parents were killed in a road accident.

Ronnie And eating alone's no fun.

Marge Well, of course, catering for four's no more trouble than catering for three.

Rose is seen coming in from the garden, talking softly to the parrot in its cage. She passes the open window during Lottie's next line

Lottie You're already catering for four, counting Rose: five, if you include the parrot.

Rose stops by the window at the mention of her name and listens

Grubb Ah, yes: I was coming to Rose. She's here to stay, then, is she?

Marge She'd need prizing off, like a barnacle.

Rose hurriedly enters the kitchen

Grubb Couldn't you explain it's all a big mistake? (*Sudden inspiration*) That you're expecting Violet back at any time?

Rose is seen listening at the slightly open door to the living-room for a while before disappearing behind it to listen further without fear of discovery

Lottie What if she took umbrage at being tossed out, and decided to make trouble? She already suspects there's something fishy about Doris's death.

Marge She'd have to be an absolute idiot *not* to! After all, Doris *did* die with a bullet through the head!

Lottie There was something in the way she mentioned that it was usually the nearest and dearest who did such things!

Ronnie She can't prove anything, though, can she?

Grubb She doesn't need to prove anything to raise suspicion and draw attention to us. A few ... indiscreet remarks ... dropped in the wrong places...

Pause

No, she'll have to go. But you certainly can't continue dumping your spare bodies in public places ... it creates a pattern for your crimes, and it's only a matter of time before someone links them.

Pause

This time it will have to be ... different.

Pause

Maybe ... if it could be done ... *openly*...

Lottie You mean a quick surreptitious push under a bus?

Pause

Grubb (*thoughtfully*) Through her shoplifting, perhaps? Where does she operate?

Marge Tesco's. She's very partial to their pork sausages.

Grubb Then nicking her would be a doddle!

Lottie But I thought that's what we wanted to avoid?

Marge It would point the bloodhounds immediately in our direction.

Grubb (*smiling*) But not if she was to hang herself in her cell before she could implicate anyone.

Lottie Oh, she'd never do——

Grubb Such things are very easily arranged. Can't you see the headlines? "Seventy year old lady, overcome with remorse at arrest for shoplifting, hangs herself in tragic act of contrition!" No problem.

Lottie But that's murder!

Grubb (*shrugging*) Well, that's one way of looking at it. On the other hand, we live in a dog-eat-dog society, so have to consider what's best for number one. Besides, ladies, just get your imaginations working: such a solution would leave us an empty room at our disposal... (*he pauses and smiles*) ...and that would give us another bite at the cherry ... if you get my drift...?

Ronnie Think of electrical appliances!

Grubb Anyway, I didn't think you ladies had any qualms about the odd body or two. Weren't you planning a similar fate for Rose, yourselves?

Marge It was still on the drawing board, so to speak. None of the finer details had been worked out.

Pause

Ronnie I think Gus has the right answer: after all, we're agreed she's gotta go. Aren't we?

Pause

Grubb Good! Then if it's settled, I'll get a special watch put on her, and we can take it from there.

Rose picks up the cage and enters the living-room

Rose Hallo, Inspector Globb; I didn't know you were here. Sorry I can't stop for a chat, but I've a couple of funerals to attend this afternoon, and a bit of shopping to do, first. At Tesco's, you know. Polly's had no breakfast, and I can't give him anything from the kitchen: he has a very delicate constitution, and I shudder to think of his reaction if I offered him a stale garibaldi!

Rose goes through the hall and into her room

Marge I don't suppose you're looking for a hangman down at that jail of yours?

The stage darkens

SCENE 4

One week later. Evening

Rose sits, pen in hand, with Lottie's novel before her. The parrot cage sits on the sideboard

Rose Now pay attention, Polly! (*She peers beneath the cloth*) And it's no good pretending to be asleep! (*She reads as she writes*) "Sergeant Gus Gimbo cast his eyes over Phyllida's seductive curves, and said huskily, 'So they were all in on it, were they, doll? Well, Caramba Legree's not going to like that no more than a hole in the head!' A grim smile illuminated his rugged features. 'She'll figure they all have to be rubbed out, won't she, babe?' 'Yeah: she sure will,' Phyllida replied, her voice a bunch of iron filings, 'and it's our sacred dooty as cops on the beat to avoid a massacre in our precinct!'"

The front doorbell rings

Rose closes the book and goes to the door to admit Grace, a woman of similar age, dressed in black. They peck cheeks and Grace looks around the room

Grace, love! I'm so glad you could make it. Take off your coat. Gawd! it's been a busy day!

Grace (*taking off her coat*) Nice little place you've got here. I came as soon as I got your note. How's Polly?

Rose takes her coat, hangs it in the hall, and re-enters

Rose A bundle of nerves as usual.

Grace How's his singing coming along?

Rose As well as can be expected, I suppose.

Grace For a parrot, you mean?

Rose It could be the curry.

Grace What curry?

Rose The Indian food I'm giving him. It's all due to having to change my shopping habits. Mr Patel sells things which, under normal circumstances, no decent parrot should be subjected to in a million years!

Grace You should have enquired as to what Indians feed their parrots on.

Rose pours a couple of sherries and hands one to Grace

Talking of altering one's shopping habits—thank heavens you warned me about Tesco's when you did. The place has been alive with detectives ever since. They caught poor old Sophie, you know.

Rose Can't say I'm surprised: she was always a little slipshod. But, of course, she was self-taught, you know.

Slight pause

Grace Are you serious about me coming to live here, like you said in your note?

Rose Of course! It may not be a palace, Grace, but it's a *home*! Besides, you've been a very good friend to me over the past twelve years, so why shouldn't you share in my good fortune?

Grace Good fortune?

Rose More of that later. How was this afternoon's funeral?

Grace (*shrugging*) So-so.

Rose And the floral tributes?

Grace Well-intended. The widow jumped down the hole on to the coffin.

Rose I once had two of those in a single month.

Grace Drunk?

Rose One was, certainly. I suspect the other, who happened to be the widow, to have been pushed by Father Richard, who felt she was trying to upstage him!

Grace You mentioned something about … a co-operative.

Rose Yes. A worker's co-operative. It's a sharing of funds … responsibilities … work. And I thought we'd combine it with a sort of … guild of shoplifters-cum-funeral-aficionados. Might even plan a few shoplifters' seminars.

Grace Sounds fantastic! But what do the others say?

Rose Oh, you don't have to worry about them!

Grace (*indicating Lottie's novel*) What's this? A diary?

Rose A novel-cum-autobiography. (*She opens it and reads*) "Gus knew that Caramba Legree was not a doll to be trifled with. Honky-tonk blues singer, gun-runner and spouse-slayer, she would prove one hell of a broad to brush with."

Grace You've sort of … disguised yourself?

Rose Vaguely.

Grace I had no idea you wrote novels.

Rose I'm finishing it for an absent friend. I've tried copying her style, to the best of my ability, but I'm not much of a writer.

Grace Nor was she, if that's anything to go by!

Rose D'you think this sounds better? "She would prove one hell of a broad to *pussy-foot* with"?

Grace I wouldn't know how to pussy-foot. I haven't learned a new dance since the twist. (*She sips her sherry*)

Rose (*reading*) "Revenge was the name of the game, Caramba felt. She'd been besmirched: betrayed."

Grace I was besmirched and betrayed, once. It was not a pleasant sensation, I assure you.

Rose stares at her coldly

Sorry. Caramba's Revenge!

Rose (*reading*) "She musingly sucked in her ivory cheeks and hissed menacingly, 'But they'll get theirs, buster. In spades! Just see if they don't!' And she jabbed the air viciously with her gold, sapphire-encrusted cigarette holder."

Grace How had she been besmirched and betrayed?

Rose They were preparing to bump her off. Ice her!

Grace Who?

Rose Four stool-pigeons she had looked upon as friends. People she had trusted!

Grace Why were they——?

Rose They saw her as a threat to them.

Grace My betrayal was when I caught my Les behind the cricket pavilion teaching Mavis Berry how to bowl a googly. (*She sips her drink*) Do you think we could go and look at the rest of the house?

Rose Later. I'm waiting for the nine o'clock news. (*She continues reading*) "Gus knew that for Caramba to succeed in her diabolical revenge, she must find an opportunity to get her enemies together, in one place, like Al Capone got Moran's gang in that garage for the Saint Valentine's Day Massacre. Unsuspecting, and at ease, they'd need to be, and though Gus knew the dirty rats deserved all that was coming to them, he must, as a cop, stop Caramba. 'You gotta realize, kid,' he told her, giddy with Fifth Avenue Zombie, her heady perfume, 'that this is *me* as a cop that is talking to *you* as one sumptuous broad that is about to break the law. But me as a red-blooded guy is a different kettle of tea!'"

Pause

Do you think Amy would be interested in joining us?

Pause

Grace I've not given it much thought, really.

Rose I mean, her being a funeral-buff, and shoplifter, like ourselves, I thought she might be quite an asset to our little operation.

Grace Don't forget she has a dog, Electra.

Rose He'd present no problem: Polly doesn't mind dogs. It's cats he's allergic to. Has a touch of asthma, I think, on top of all his other worries. We must think seriously about it. (*She continues reading*) "Suddenly Caramba smiled a secret, triumphant smile, her tempting lips twitching with anticipation and excitement. She had found the perfect time and place for her revenge! Her beautiful green eyes glittered with savage passion as she nonchalantly whistled a few bars from *The Teddy Bears Picnic*, visualising the bodies of her four deadliest foes, limbs akimbo, in their final grotesque dance of death!"

Grace I hate to interrupt, but it's gone nine o'clock.

Rose Why didn't you tell me? (*She crosses and switches on the television*)

Grace I didn't want——

Rose Sssshhh!

TV ...more news on the car that went over a cliff this afternoon, containing four passengers, of whom there are no survivors...

Grace (*pointing to the screen*) But that's the——
Rose Sssshhh! (*She sits smugly grinning through the news bulletin*)
TV ...it is thought, from items discovered at the scene of the tragedy, that the car's occupants were there on a picnic, and that a faulty handbrake was the probable cause of its fatal plunge on to the needle-sharp rocks below. An earlier report of an elderly woman seen leaving the scene of the accident has not been confirmed, nor has anyone come forward. Now for a summary of the main points of the news——

Rose switches off the set

Grace That was the exact spot your Sidney went to meet his Maker, wasn't it? (*She looks at Rose and laughs*)
Rose The very same.
Grace Rose! You didn't...? (*She continues laughing*)
Rose The handbrake wasn't faulty: it was very stiff, as a matter of fact.
Grace You were truly inspired, Rose! An act of pure genius!
Rose (*modestly*) Oh, I didn't do it *entirely* alone, Grace. Even the best laid plans of mice and men need a little assistance from the Almighty. And just as I was despairing of ever getting them off the grass and back in the car together, He sent a short, sharp shower, to send them scampering into the car for cover. Ah, I thought, that's surely a sign of heaven's approval! (*She shrugs*) Then it was simply a matter of slipping the handbrake ... a slight push... (*She smiles modestly*) ...and the rest is legend!
Grace (*laughing*) So that was Caramba's revenge?
Rose I shall, of course, attend the final transmission of their souls: incognito, I think. Perhaps a small floral tribute from an anonymous mourner.
Grace I approve of that, Rose. It has class!
Rose A few violets, perhaps? Something ... discreet and understated. (*A smile, as she considers this*) Oh, and talking of violets, there's one little obstacle. No more than a technical hitch, really. You see, this house is in the name of a woman named Violet, and I think it might be ... safer ... for me to become Violet...
Grace (*cheerfully*) Well, you know what they say? A rose by any other name...
Rose Also, I need an alibi for this afternoon.
Grace Simple: we say we went to the cinema. And saw *Terminator Two*!

Rose smiles. There is a slight pause as she looks around the place fondly

Rose D'you know, Grace, from the very first time I set eyes on this place, I felt it to be my ... destiny.
Grace Don't you think that ought to go into your book, dear?

Rose Perhaps you're right. (*She opens Lottie's novel, and reads as she writes*) "Caramba Legree surveyed the walls, as she pulled her oyster satin kimono across her pale alabaster thighs, and sucked at her Turkish cigarette. 'Every goddam brick in this mausoleum is one hell of a part of my destiny,' she told herself, her classic bosom heaving with pent-up emotion..."

The stage darkens

FURNITURE AND PROPERTY LIST

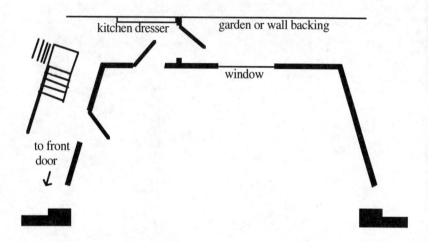

kitchen dresser   garden or wall backing

window

to front
door
↓

Further dressing may be added at the director's discretion

ACT I

SCENE 1

On stage: Sideboard with drawers containing revolver, minutes book.
        On it: drinks including sherry, glasses, clock, cash box,
        accounts book
        Table. *On it:* pen, excercise book
        4 chairs
        Television
        Shopping trolley. *In it:* groceries including small jar
        Part of kitchen with units and utensils can be seen

Off stage: Watering can (**Doris**)
        2 black and white photographs (**Lottie**)

Personal: **Lottie:** pocket calculator
        Doris: change

SCENE 2

On stage: As before

Personal: **Marge:** coat, hat

SCENE 3

On stage: As before

Set: **Marge**'s knitting

Off stage: Tray containing cups, etc. (**Lottie**)
Tea (**Lottie**)

SCENE 4

On stage: As before

Set: Cutlery and crockery
Napkins

Off stage: Screw-top coffee jar, containing ice and ingredients for
martinis (**Marge**)

Personal: **Ronnie:** kerchief, large brass ear-rings, notes

ACT II

SCENE 1

On stage: As before

Off stage: Screw-top coffee jar (**Marge**)
Tureen of soup, bread (**Marge**)

Personal: **Lottie:** notebook
Grubb: notebook, ballpoint pen, watch

SCENE 2

On stage: As before

Strike:	**Marge**'s screw-top coffee jar
	Tureen of soup
	Bread

Off stage:	Tray with three cups of coffee (**Ronnie**)
	Coffee, biscuits (**Ronnie**)
	Small case, birdcage covered with cloth (**Rose**)

| *Personal:* | **Grubb:** notebook |
| | **Grubb:** plastic bag containing revolver |

SCENE 3

| *On stage:* | As before |

| *Off stage:* | Pension book (**Rose**) |
| | Cage (**Rose**) |

SCENE 4

| *On stage:* | As before |

| *Set:* | Parrot cage on sideboard |

| *Personal:* | **Grace:** coat |

LIGHTING PLOT

Property fittings required: nil
Interior. The same throughout

ACT I, SCENE 1

To open: Overall general lighting

Cue 1   The pinger sounds in the kitchen   (Page 12)
             Fade lights down

ACT I, SCENE 2

To open: Overall general lighting

Cue 2   **Lottie** leads **Ronnie** off   (Page 19)
             Fade lights down

ACT I, SCENE 3

To open: Overall morning lighting

Cue 3   **Lottie** begins writing in her book   (Page 30)
             Fade lights down

ACT I, SCENE 4

To open: Overall evening lighting

Cue 4   **Marge** switches TV on   (Page 38)
             Bring up TV effect, continuing

Cue 5   **TV**: "…the areas worst hit…"   (Page 38)
             Fade lights and TV down

ACT II, SCENE 1

To open: Overall evening lighting and TV effect

Cue 6   **Marge** switches TV off   (Page 39)
             Cut TV effect

Cue 7   **Marge**: "…a nice tomato rinse, then?"   (Page 50)
             Fade lights down

ACT II, SCENE 2

To open: Overall morning lighting

Cue 8   **Lottie** and **Marge** burst into laughter   (Page 57)
             Fade lights down

ACT II, SCENE 3

To open: Overall general lighting

Cue 9   **Marge**: "…down at that jail of yours?"   (Page 64)
             Fade lights down

ACT II, SCENE 4

To open: Overall evening lighting

Cue 10   **Rose** switches TV on   (Page 67)
             Bring up TV effect, continuing

Cue 11   **Rose** switches TV off   (Page 68)
             Cut TV effect

Cue 12   **Rose**: "…heaving with pent-up emotion…"   (Page 69)
             Fade lights down

EFFECTS PLOT

ACT I

ACT II

Cue 12	At start of Act II *Doorbell rings; TV voice in background*	(Page 39)
Cue 13	**Marge** switches TV off *Cut TV voice*	(Page 39)
Cue 14	**Marge**: "…blue rinse fighting to get out." *Doorbell rings*	(Page 43)
Cue 15	At start of Scene 2 *Clock strikes three-quarters*	(Page 50)
Cue 16	**Marge**: "And think of electrical appliances!" *Doorbell rings*	(Page 54)
Cue 17	**Marge**: "…intends doing about it?" *Doorbell rings*	(Page 57)
Cue 18	**Rose**: "…avoid a massacre in our precinct!" *Doorbell rings*	(Page 65)
Cue 19	**Rose** switches TV on *TV voice as script page 68*	(Page 67)
Cue 20	**Rose** switches TV off *Cut TV voice*	(Page 68)